A 21st Century Budget Process for California

**Recommendations of the
California Citizens Budget Commission**

Copies of this report and the Center's previous reports are available from the Center. Send order to the publisher, Center for Governmental Studies, 10951 West Pico Boulevard, Suite 120, Los Angeles, California 90064, or call (310) 470-6590 or send e-mail to center@cgs.org.

Library of Congress Catalog Card Number: 98-85611

ISBN: 0-9664648-0-X

Dedication

To Christine Reed

The untimely death of Christine Reed was a great loss to the members and staff of the California Citizens Budget Commission, as it was to so many other individuals and organizations, public and private, to whom Chris gave so much of her time and effort. Her cheerfulness and optimism always buoyed and brightened the Commission meetings in which she participated.

Equally valuable was the practicality and common sense she brought to all discussions of the complex and often contentious issues which were the subject matter of the Commission's activities. We feel privileged to have had her participation in our deliberations and miss greatly the continuing contributions she would surely have made to the publication of this report.

Other Publications of the Center for Governmental Studies

A State of Learning: California and the Dream of Higher Education in the 21ˢᵗ Century, California Citizen's Commission on Higher Education (1998)

The Democracy Network (www.dnet.org), an interactive system of political communication and information on the World Wide Web for elections in California and other states, Center for Governmental Studies (1996)

Opportunity Through Technology: A Conference on New Communication Technology and Low-Income Communities, Connect LA (1997)

A Shared Vision: A Practical Guide to the Design and Implementation of a Performance-Based Budget Model for California State Health Services, California Citizens Budget Commission (1997)

Promises to Keep and Miles to Go: A Summary of the Joint Meeting of the California Citizen's Commission on Higher Education and the California Education Roundtable (1997)

Campaign Money on the Information Superhighway: Electronic Filing and Disclosure of Campaign Finance Reports, National Resource Center for State and Local Campaign Finance Reform (1996, 1997)

The Price of Justice: A Los Angeles Area Case Study in Judicial Campaign Financing, California Commission on Campaign Financing (1995)

Reforming California's Budget Process: Preliminary Report and Recommendations, California Citizens Budget Commission (1995)

The Democracy Network: Interactive Multimedia Prototype for an Electronic Voter Information System, Center for Governmental Studies (1994-1995)

California at the Crossroads: Choices for Health Care Reform, Lucien Wulsin, Jr. (1994)

Democracy by Initiative: Shaping California's Fourth Branch of Government, California Commission on Campaign Financing (1992)

To Govern Ourselves: Ballot Initiatives in the Los Angeles Area, California Commission on Campaign Financing (1992)

Money and Politics in the Golden State: Financing California's Local Elections, California Commission on Campaign Financing (1989)

Money and Politics in Local Elections: The Los Angeles Area, California Commission on Campaign Financing (1989)

The California Channel: A New Public Affairs Television Network for the State, Tracy Westen and Beth Givens (1989)

Update to the New Gold Rush, California Commission on Campaign Financing (1987)

The New Gold Rush: Financing California's Legislative Campaigns, California Commission on Campaign Financing (1985)

Table of Contents

Part I

Overview of California's Budget Procedures   **9**

Part IV

Appendices

Tables and Charts

Foreword

The California Citizens Budget Commission is a nonprofit, bipartisan, private organization formed in 1993. Twenty-five Californians from the State's business, labor, academic, judicial, civic and public service sectors, including Democrats, Independents and Republicans, have volunteered their time and talents to serve as Commission members. The Commission is a project of the Center for Governmental Studies, a non-profit, non-partisan, tax exempt organization which researches, designs and helps implement innovative approaches to improve the processes of government in California and across the nation.

Over the past four years, the Commission has examined the budgeting practices of California and other states, interviewed a large number of elected officials, legislative and administrative staff and budgetary experts, and canvassed the existing literature on state budget practices. The Commission has identified a wide range of problems afflicting California's budgeting process. These include lack of a true balanced-budget requirement, requiring a two-thirds majority for budget passage, excessive use of "off-budget" transactions obscuring the State's true fiscal condition, lack of timely public access to key budget information, repeated attempts to gloss over long-term fiscal problems with short-term "quick fix" solutions, and lack of accountability in the state budget process.

The Commission has developed a comprehensive set of recommendations which—if implemented by the Governor, the Legislature and, where necessary, the voters—could significantly reform California's budgeting process and substantially reduce many of the State's current budget difficulties. **A list of the Commission's recommendations is included in the Executive Summary of this report. Proposed constitutional and statutory changes needed to implement the recommendations are included as Appendix J.**

This report summarizes the budgeting problems the Commission has identified and the recommendations it has proposed. The Commission's recommendations are not intended to affect the State's substantive budgetary decisions—such as how much money should be spent on education or corrections, or whether specific taxes should be increased or cut. Substantive decisions on the proper levels of spending for particular programs are political decisions which will continue to be made, as they properly should be, by the Governor, the Legislature and the electorate, in accordance with their policy judgments (which are beyond the purview of the Commission and this report).

The Commission has designed its recommendations only to reshape California's budgeting *process* – that decision-making *system* used by the State to allocate its fiscal resources. If fully implemented, the Commission believes that its recommendations, as set forth in this report, could not only greatly improve the overall state budget process, but also be a major factor in putting an end to the constant deadlock and delay that is, unfortunately, the hallmark of the State's current budgetary procedure.

Acknowledgments

The Commission extends its warm appreciation to the James Irvine Foundation, the William and Flora Hewlett Foundation and the Sierra Health Foundation for their generous support, without which this project could not have been undertaken.

The Commission also extends its special thanks to Directors of Finance Russell S. Gould and Craig L. Brown and their staffs, and to Legislative Analyst Elizabeth G. Hill and her staff, for the information and commentary they made available to this project. Thanks are also due to the staffs of the fiscal committees in the Legislature, to Assemblyman Robert M. Hertzberg and his staff (in particular, the work on various budget issues done at his request by the Office of the Legislative Counsel) and to Senator Quentin L. Kopp and his staff.

In addition, we express our appreciation to the staffs of numerous local government agencies and organizations concerned with state fiscal matters, in particular the California Budget Project, the California Governance Consensus Project, the California State Association of Counties, the California Taxpayers Association and the League of California Cities.

The Commission is deeply grateful to Professors Elizabeth Garrett and Theodore P. Seto who provided their advice and suggestions to the Commission and its staff in the preparation of this report. Professor Seto also obtained for the Commission the assistance of student interns at Loyola Law School, in particular senior law student Adam A. Phipps, whose diligent research made possible the Appendices to this report.

The Commission also expresses special gratitude to its dedicated staff. Executive Director Alexander H. Pope and former Project Directors Susan North and Kevin Scott, with the able assistance of Center President Tracy Westen and General Counsel Robert M. Stern, assisted the Commission in its deliberations and in the preparation of this report. Craig B. Holman, Karen Klabin, Nicolas B. Schweizer and Matthew T. Stodder assisted with substantive research. Susan Clizbe, Nadine Rochler and Linda Watson prepared the report for publication. Robert Herstek designed the report's cover.

The California Citizens Budget Commission

Co-Chairs

Lisa Foster – Of Counsel, Phillips and Cohen; Adjunct Professor of Law, University of San Diego. Formerly: Executive Director, California Common Cause; staff attorney, Legal Aid Foundation of Los Angeles and Center for Law in the Public Interest.

Robert T. Monagan – Past President, California Economic Development Corporation. Formerly: Assemblyman and Speaker of the California Assembly; Assistant Secretary of the U.S. Department of Transportation.

A. Alan Post – Chair, Citizens Commission on Ballot Initiatives. Formerly: Legislative Analyst, State of California; Chair, Commission on Government Reform.

Members

John A. Arguelles – Justice, California Supreme Court (Retired); Of Counsel, Gibson, Dunn & Crutcher; Vice Chairman, Independent Commission to Study Los Angeles Police Department Practices.

Nancy Bekavac – President, Scripps College. Formerly: Counsel to the President of Dartmouth College; Executive Director of the Thomas Watson Foundation; Partner, Munger, Tolles and Olson in Los Angeles.

Melinda R. Bird – Managing Attorney, Protection and Advocacy, Inc., Los Angeles Office. Formerly: Attorney, Western Center on Law and Poverty, Inc.; Honoree, William O. Douglas Award Dinner, Public Counsel/Los Angeles County and Beverly Hills Bar Associations.

Ward Connerly – President and Principal Consultant, Connerly & Associates, Inc.; Regent, University of California; member, Council on California Competitiveness. Formerly: Chief Deputy Director, Department of Housing & Community Development; Chief Consultant, Assembly Committee on Housing & Community Development.

Dan Garcia – Senior Vice President, Corporate Real Estate, Warner Bros. and Warner Music Group; Trustee, The Rockefeller Foundation; Board of Directors, Kaiser Foundation Hospitals and Health Plans. Formerly: President, Los Angeles City Airport Commission; President, City of Los Angeles Planning Commission;

President, City of Los Angeles Police Commission; Chairman, Greater Los Angeles Chamber of Commerce; Chairman, Los Angeles Community Redevelopment Agency; President, Mexican-American Bar Association.

Walter B. Gerken – Chairman of the Equity Board, PIMCO Advisors L.P.; Chairman, The Executive Service Corps of Southern California; Member, The California Citizens Commission on Higher Education. Formerly: Supervisor of Budget and Administrative Analysis for the State of Wisconsin; Chairman, California Business Roundtable; Chairman, California Nature Conservancy; Chairman and CEO, Pacific Mutual Life Insurance Company.

Wilford D. Godbold, Jr. – President and Chief Executive Officer, ZERO Corporation; member, Council on California Competitiveness; Chairman, Public Affairs Council, California Chamber of Commerce. Formerly: Chairman, Board of Directors, California Chamber of Commerce; Chairman, Board of Directors, The Employers Group; Partner, Gibson, Dunn & Crutcher.

William G. Hamm – Principal, Law & Economics Consulting Group, Inc. Formerly: Executive Vice President and Chief Operating Officer, Federal Home Loan Bank of San Francisco; Vice President, World Savings and Loan; Legislative Analyst, State of California; Deputy Associate Director, U.S. Office of Management and Budget/ Executive Office of the President.

Phillip L. Isenberg – Of Counsel, Hyde, Miller, Owen & Trost; Lecturer in the Public Policy and Administration program, California State University, Sacramento. Formerly: California State Assemblyman; Member, California Constitution Revision Commission; Mayor of Sacramento; Sacramento City Councilman.

Stewart Kwoh – Executive Director, Asian Pacific American Legal Center of Southern California; Instructor, University of California, Los Angeles; Trustee, The California Endowment and The California Wellness Foundation. Formerly: member, Rebuild L.A.; President, Southern California Chinese Lawyers Association; Commissioner and President, Los Angeles City Human Relations Commission.

Cornell Maier – Chairman and Chief Executive Officer (Retired), Kaiser Aluminum & Chemical Corporation; Consultant, Kaiser Aluminum Corporation; member, Educational Task Force, California Business Roundtable. Formerly: Director, California Leadership; Director/Executive Committee Member, Bay Area Council.

Burt Pines – Senior Partner, Alschuler Grossman & Pines LLP; Special Counsel to Los Angeles City Mayor Richard Riordan; Board of Directors, Los Angeles Area Chamber of Commerce. Formerly: City Attorney of Los Angeles; Judge Pro Tem, Beverly Hills Municipal Court; Member, California Council on Criminal Justice; Assistant United States Attorney, Criminal Division, Los Angeles; Board of Directors, Constitutional Rights Foundation; Trustee, National Institute of Municipal Law Offices.

Virgil Roberts – Managing Partner, Bobbitt and Roberts; Chairman, Los Angeles Annenberg Metropolitan Project; Vice Chairman, California Community Foundation; Vice Chairman, Public Education Network. Formerly: President, Solar Records.

Elizabeth Davis Rogers – Managing General Partner, Pacific Earth Resources; member, Council for California Competitiveness.

Kevin Scott – Principal, Strategies for Changing Times. Formerly: Project Director, California Citizens Budget Commission; Vice President, Goldman, Sachs & Co.; Executive Director, Commission on State Finance; Lecturer, John F. Kennedy School of Government, Harvard University.

Rocco C. Siciliano – Chairman, The Dwight D. Eisenhower World Affairs Institute; Chairman of the Board, Center for Governmental Studies; Trustee, Committee for Economic Development, New York; Director, United Television, Inc.; retired Chairman, Ticor, Inc., Los Angeles. Formerly: Chairman, California Business Roundtable; Special Assistant to President Eisenhower; Under Secretary, U.S. Department of Commerce; Assistant Secretary, U.S. Department of Labor.

Richard P. Simpson – President (Retired), California Taxpayers' Association. Formerly: County Administrator, Yuba and El Dorado counties; author, "California Counties on the Fiscal Fault Line" for the County Supervisors' Association.

Harry Sunderland – Vice Chairman (Retired) and Consultant, Safeway, Inc.; Task Force Co-Chairman, California Business Roundtable; Vice-Chairman, Californians for Compensation Reform; member, Council on California Competitiveness.

Paul M. Varacalli – International Vice President, Service Employees International Union, AFL-CIO; Executive Director, SEIU Local 790; Member, State Job Training Coordinating Council; Chair, UC Berkeley Labor Advisory Committee; instructor of labor courses, University of California and community colleges.

Francis M. Wheat – Advisory Partner and former Senior Partner, Gibson, Dunn & Crutcher; Co-Chairman, California Commission on Campaign Financing. Formerly: Commissioner, U.S. Securities and Exchange Commission; President, Los Angeles County Bar Association.

Harold M. Williams – Director, Public Policy Institute of California; Director, California Endowment; Co-chair, California Citizens Commission on Higher Education. Formerly: President and Chief Executive Officer, J. Paul Getty Trust; Chairman, U.S. Securities and Exchange Commission; Dean, UCLA Anderson Graduate School of Management; Chairman, Norton Simon, Inc.; Board of Directors, Times-Mirror Corp.; Board of Directors, Sun America, Inc.; Trustee, Committee for Economic Development.

Alison A. Winter – President and Chief Executive Officer, Northern Trust Bank; Chair, Los Angeles Area Chamber of Commerce; member, Executive Committee, Board of Visitors, UCLA Anderson Graduate School of Management; Director, California HealthCare Foundation; Director, YMCA of Metropolitan Los Angeles;

Director, The Employers Group. Formerly: Chairman, Asset Management Committee, American Bankers Association Trust Division; Director and President, Investment Analysts Society of Chicago; Director, Financial Analysts Federation; Governor, Los Angeles Society of Financial Analysts.

Staff

Alexander H. Pope – Executive Director, California Citizens Budget Commission. Formerly: Los Angeles County Assessor; Legislative Secretary to Governor Edmund G. Brown, Sr.; Member and President, Los Angeles Airport Commission; Member, California Highway Commission; practicing attorney in Los Angeles for more than 30 years.

Tracy Westen – President, Center for Governmental Studies; Executive Director, California Commission on Campaign Financing; Adjunct Professor of Law, USC-Annenberg School for Communication; Lecturer, UCLA Law School; President, The Democracy Network. Formerly: Founder and Vice President, The California Channel; Deputy Director, Federal Trade Commission, Washington, D.C.

Robert M. Stern – General Counsel, California Citizens Budget Commission; Co-Director and General Counsel, California Commission on Campaign Financing; Staff Director, Council on Governmental Ethics Laws; Lecturer, UCLA. Formerly: General Counsel, California Fair Political Practices Commission; principal co-author of Political Reform Act of 1974 (Proposition 9).

Karen Klabin – Policy Coordinator, Human Services Network, Los Angeles. Formerly: Research Analyst, California Citizens Budget Commission; political columnist, Los Angeles View; Art Editor, Detour Magazine; freelance journalist for national and local publications.

Craig B. Holman, Ph.D. – Senior Researcher, Center for Governmental Studies; Project Manager, National Resource Center on State and Local Campaign Finance Reform. Formerly: Senior Researcher, Jesse M. Unruh Institute of Politics at the University of Southern California.

Matthew T. Stodder – Electronic Editor, Los Angeles Times. Formerly: Project Director, The Democracy Network; Data Analysis Project Manager, California Commission on Campaign Finance Reform; Intern, California Legislature.

Part I

Executive Summary

Executive Summary

California's annual state budget embodies the most important decisions made by our state government. The budget is the tool with which state officials manage the spending of more than $100 billion of state and federal funds each year. Although little understood by the public, the state budget vitally affects the lives of all Californians.

Many aspects of California's state budget process follow the best practices of modern public finance. In other ways, however, the budget process falls far short of today's needs. Most basically, there is no constitutional requirement that the budget be balanced when it is passed by the Legislature and signed by the Governor. Equally important, adoption of the budget requires a two-thirds vote in both houses of the Legislature, allowing small minorities in either house to frustrate the process of reaching the compromises essential to budget passage and obscuring responsibility for fiscal decision-making. In addition, the budget process does not give average citizens the information and understanding they need to exercise effective democratic control and hold responsible elected officials properly accountable for the spending of the vast public resources allocated annually in the state budget.

Despite their widely diverse backgrounds and experiences, the Commission members were able to reach consensus on these proposed reforms by considering a great variety of suggested changes and recommending only those with respect to which there was general agreement. They are convinced that these proposed reforms, while not resolving the constant political tensions that inevitably accompany the state budget process, will nevertheless markedly improve both the manner in which the State's budget is adopted and also the public's understanding of the budget process and acceptance of its results.

The Commission's Findings

California should balance its state budget more rigorously.

The California Constitution charges the Governor with the responsibility of presenting a balanced budget to the Legislature each January, but does not require that the final enacted budget be balanced. The Commission believes that California's budget should be in balance as presented, as passed by the Legislature, and as signed into law by the Governor.

The failure to follow a balanced-budget policy can lead to a breakdown in fiscal discipline. Allowing even a few deficit spending expenditures makes it that much more difficult to reject the other spending requests that will inevitably follow. Repeated deficits, however limited, accumulate and, especially if combined with economic hard times, can lead to severe budgetary distress and inadequate funding for truly vital public services. The Commission recommends that California join the great majority of states that have constitutional balanced-budget requirements.[1]

In addition, the Joint Legislative Budget Committee should monitor the progress of the budget during the fiscal cycle and make necessary recommendations for keeping the budget in balance. In default of such legislative action, the Governor should have the authority to reduce expenditures to maintain the balance.

Related measures needed for California to implement a policy of proper fiscal discipline include limiting borrowing to finance deficit spending, prohibiting the use of "off-budget" transactions to avoid balanced-budget requirements (see footnote), and requiring that long-term borrowing be used only to finance capital expenditures.

The state budget process should be governed by majority vote.

California is one of only two states that require a two-thirds vote of both houses of the Legislature to pass the budget under all circumstances. Defended as a restraint on spending, there is no clear evidence that this supermajority requirement does, in fact, have that effect. Legislators can as easily withhold votes to secure increases in spending for their favorite programs as they can to secure spending reductions.

---

[1] States have no practical alternative to a long-term balanced budget policy. They lack the tax base, monetary controls and borrowing capacity that enable the federal government to engage in massive, continuing deficit spending. They also lack the federal government's power to control business (and population) movements across their borders. Continued deficit spending drives up financing costs and thereby taxes—resulting in a vicious circle of business (and population) flight leading to still higher taxes, more flight and so forth. Such a policy is, therefore, ultimately self-defeating. For these reasons, private financial markets will not provide credit for continued state deficit spending, a practical lesson brought painfully home to California budget makers during the recent recession.

Rather than holding down spending, the two-thirds vote requirement places the power to control or block the budget into the hands of a small minority in either house of the Legislature—thereby promoting gridlock and enhancing special interest group influence. It also allows political parties in the Legislature to avoid responsibility for unpopular budget decisions and blame them on others. The public is left finding it difficult to hold anyone, including the Governor, responsible.

For these reasons, the Commission recommends that the state budget be adopted by a majority vote, the same vote required for most major actions by the Legislature. The Commission believes that the present limitations on the state budget process are such that the additional requirement of a two-thirds vote is not necessary. The state budget does not create new programs, it simply determines the spending levels for previously authorized programs for the period of a single year. In addition, the Governor's line-item veto authority is available to restrain the pet project appropriations that may result from legislative deal making.

For the same policy reasons, the Commission further recommends that the majority vote requirement should be applied to the budget implementation bills that accompany and are signed simultaneously with the budget.

An anomalous situation exists with respect to the vote requirements for the creation and repeal of tax preferences (such as tax deductions, credits and deferrals), often referred to as "tax expenditures." At present, tax expenditures can be created by simple majority votes in the Legislature, but can only be repealed by two-thirds votes. The difficulty in eliminating such tax preferences accounts, in part, for their proliferation in California's Revenue and Taxation Code. The Commission believes that this disparate treatment should be ended, and that tax expenditures should be both created and repealed by majority vote.

More generally, the constitutional and statutory provisions governing the state budget process are replete with constraints on the power of the Governor and the Legislature to allocate and spend state revenue in accordance with current public needs and preferences. Only a small fraction of state spending is discretionary, that is, controlled by the Legislature and the Governor solely in terms of current needs as they see them.

The Commission recommends that all budget constraints should be regularly reviewed in their entirety by the Joint Legislative Budget Committee. In addition, during each gubernatorial term a citizens commission, similar to the California Constitution Revision Commission, should be formed to conduct a comprehensive review of the constraints and make recommendations for appropriate modifications. To give added weight to those recommendations, the Commission believes that the Legislature, acting by majority vote, should have the power to place those recommendations involving constitutional amendments on the ballot for action by the voters.

The state budget process should be comprehensive, accessible and long-term oriented.

California's current budget process is incomplete. Large amounts of federal and local resources which finance state programs, in part, are not included in the state budget. Tax expenditures are also not included in the process. The Commission recommends that the State have a unified and comprehensive state budget process. All program expenditures, revenues and tax expenditures (including all federal and local fiscal involvement in state programs) should be incorporated in that process.

Although the state's budget process produces massive amounts of information, too little of it is summarized in a form that can be easily understood by interested members of the public. Voters cannot participate in making difficult fiscal decisions unless the underlying information is accessible to them. The Commission recommends that the Budget Act itself contain a summary of all important budget information. In addition, the State should make an easily understood budget summary widely available to the public, and should distribute a budget primer to all taxpayers annually. Further, the State needs to be ready to adjust its budget procedures for dealing with public input for the day when communication via the Internet and other electronic means will be the norm.

California's annual budget process is currently too focused on the short-term aspects of state spending. Major programs, in particular the so-called Big Five programs (K-12 education, health, social services, corrections and higher education) on which more than 90% of General Fund moneys are spent, do not lend themselves to quick fixes or short-term solutions. Many knowledgeable observers are convinced that long-term economic growth is dependent on long-term investment in the State's human resources and infrastructure. For these reasons, the Commission believes that the state budget should contain a long-term spending plan (including a capital improvement budget) and that the State should shift to a two-year budget cycle as soon as possible.

Accountability should be built into the state budget process.

At present, California spends large sums on a wide range of programs, many of which lack clearly defined goals. Also, the State applies few measures of program effectiveness to its spending programs. To remedy this situation, the Commission recommends that performance goals and objectives should be included in the state budget, and that the budget should also contain specific measures of program performance and effectiveness, wherever possible, for all programs and agencies. Such requirements would substantially improve the ability of interested citizens to determine whether State programs are achieving their stated purposes and being operated in a cost-effective manner.

The Commission's Recommendations

California should balance its state budget more rigorously.

1. All future state budgets—as presented by the Governor, passed by the Legislature and signed by the Governor—should be required to have a balanced General Fund. Budgeted General Fund expenditures should not exceed estimated revenues for the budget cycle.

2. External borrowing to finance a deficit should be prohibited, except to meet legitimate cash flow needs within the current and immediately succeeding budget year. Roll-over of such short-term debt to any later budget year should occur only in the event of defined emergency circumstances voted by a 60% majority of both houses of the Legislature.

3. Long-term debt should be limited to capital items.

4. Off-budget state expenditures and borrowing should be constitutionally prohibited.

5. During both legislative sessions and interim periods, the Joint Legislative Budget Committee should have the responsibility of recommending any legislative actions needed to keep the budget in balance. In the absence of corrective action by the Legislature, the Governor should have the authority to make such expenditure reductions as are needed to maintain the balance.

The state budget process should be governed by majority vote.

6. The state budget should be enacted by simple majority vote of the two houses of the Legislature.

7. Budget implementation bills should be treated as part of the state budget (adopted by majority vote, subject to the line-item veto and not limited by the single-subject rule).

8. Tax expenditures should be created, modified or repealed in accordance with the same vote requirement: a majority vote of the Legislature.

9. In even-numbered years, the legislative session should have a period of time, beginning June 1 and ending with the passage of the Budget Act, when adoption of the Budget would be the only order of business.

10. In every budget cycle, the Joint Legislative Budget Committee should review and issue a report on the fiscal impacts of all constitutional and statutory expenditure and revenue constraints on the state budget process. On a quadrennial basis, an independent body should be created to conduct a similar review (to include all continuing appropriations and special funds) and recommend appropriate modifications of those constraints to the Legislature. The Legislature should be authorized, acting by majority vote, to submit to a vote of the people such of those recommendations as involve constitutional amendments.

The state budget process should be comprehensive, accessible and long-term oriented.

11. California should have a unified and comprehensive state budget process. All projected expenditures, revenues and tax expenditures (including all subventions to and transfers from other levels of government) should be included in that process.

12. The Budget Act should include:

    (a) a listing of all state tax expenditures,
    (b) a statement of the state's overall fiscal condition, and
    (c) a complete summary of estimated expenditures and revenues from all sources.

13. A final budget summary in simple language should be prepared by the Department of Finance and the Legislative Analyst's Office for wide and immediate distribution, and an easy-to-read budget primer should be included in the taxpayer material mailed out annually to all taxpayers by the Franchise Tax Board.

14. California should shift to a two-year state budget, to be adopted in even-numbered years.

15. A long-term strategic spending plan (including a prioritized capital outlay program) should be included in the Budget Act. Five-year expenditure and revenue projections should be included in the state budget documents and in all legislation with substantial fiscal impacts.

Accountability should be built into the state budget process.

16. Performance and effectiveness objectives should be part of all state budget segments.

17. The state budget should contain specific measures of program performance and effectiveness for all agencies and programs.

Overview of California's Budget Procedures

Overview of California's Budget Procedures

Introduction – A Brief Historical Perspective

A mega-state means mega-budgets.

If California were a nation rather than a state, its economy would be seventh-largest in the world. California's estimated 1997 gross state product of more than $1 trillion accounts for more than 15% of the nation's gross domestic product. Not surprisingly, given its nation-sized population and economy, California has by far the largest state budget in the country, surpassing that of the second-largest state, New York, by almost $25 billion in state funds.[2]

Despite major program reductions during the early 1990s, total spending from state taxes and other state revenues will exceed $69 billion for fiscal year 1997-98. Funding for some of California's individual programs—for example, K-12 education at $22 billion—is larger than the entire budget of most other states. During the 1997-98 fiscal year, state spending per capita is estimated to be $2,000 per person (7.67% of personal income).[3]

A recent U.S. Bureau of the Census report predicted that California's 1997 population, estimated at 33.3 million, would grow to more than 50 million by the year 2025.[4] This population growth, and the increased economic activity that will accompany it, will cause massive increases in the state budget. That growth will largely define the fiscal pressure points that will be felt by state and local governments. For example, California now has 5.6 million students attending

---

[2] New York State, *1997-98 Financial Plan, Mid-Year Update.*
[3] *Governor's Budget Summary 1997-98,* Schedule 6, page A-19. The 1998-99 data is available on the Department of Finance World Wide Web site at http://www.dof.ca.gov. From the home page, click on California Budget, then Governor's Budget Summary 1998-99, then Appendix & Schedules, then Schedule 6.
[4] U. S. Department of Commerce, Bureau of the Census, *Population Paper No. 47, Population Projections for States* (1997).

elementary and high schools.[5] If the number of school-age children grows in step with the total population, enrollment will reach 9 million by 2025—an increase of 62%—bringing with it pressure to increase state spending on schools.

The 1950s and '60s: High taxes and a high rate of spending

During the two decades following World War II, California experienced tremendous population growth and corresponding increases in revenue and state spending. The public sector played a crucial role in California's growth. Investment in the State's infrastructure—particularly in higher education, transportation and the water supply—was a paramount priority in the effort to modernize the Golden State during the post-war years. The levels of state and local taxation were correspondingly high: by the 1960s, California consistently ranked in the top 10 states in spending and in taxation (calculated on either a per capita or a percentage of income basis).[6] A first priority for newly elected governors Pat Brown (in 1959) and Ronald Reagan (in 1967) was to secure major tax increases to finance state spending during their terms in office.

The 1970s: When the tax burden grows faster than personal income, taxpayers get grumpy.

Although largely unseen at the time, public support for continued rapid budget growth was undermined by the developing perception that the State's tax system was unfair. By the mid-1970s, state and local tax revenues were growing faster than personal income, and taxpayers were becoming increasingly unhappy. Locally, inflation in home values was rapidly increasing assessed values. When local officials failed to make corresponding tax rate reductions, property taxes soared in many areas. At the State level, a large surplus was developing, primarily produced by the unanticipated impact of inflation on the newly revised brackets in the State's highly progressive personal income tax. (See Table 2.)

Lack of meaningful action by responsible elected officials to solve the problem fomented public discontent. To remedy inaction by local taxing authorities and in Sacramento, Californians turned to the initiative process, beginning a tax revolt that fundamentally changed the fiscal structure of government in California.

California's new era of fiscal restraint began in 1978 with the passage of Proposition 13, a measure designed to reduce and thereafter limit the growth in property taxes and make increases in state and local taxes more difficult. Prop. 13 required voter approval of many local tax increases and raised the vote requirement for increases in state taxes from a majority to a two-thirds vote in the

---

[5] *Governor's Budget Summary 1997-98*, page 79.
[6] U. S. Department of Commerce, Bureau of the Census, *Census of Governments* (various years).

Legislature.[7] Spurred by the large State surplus, the Governor and Legislature quickly responded with tax reductions of their own. Within two years, they had repealed the business inventory tax and sponsored a ballot measure that repealed the inheritance tax. In two additional initiatives, the voters imposed constitutional limits on state and local government spending and permanently indexed the state income tax to inflation.[8]

Four consecutive governors—Ronald Reagan, Jerry Brown, George Deukmejian and Pete Wilson—preached fiscal restraint. There were no major tax hikes during the terms of Governors Brown and Deukmejian. Yet during that 16-year period of stable tax rates, new spending obligations were undertaken (a significant portion of which was comprised of "bail out" subventions to local governments to partially replace the reduction in property tax revenues resulting from Proposition 13) which far exceeded the offsetting impact of the program cuts made at that time. This resulted in a "structural imbalance" which plagued budget-makers in later years, especially during the recession of the early 1990s.

The 1980s and 90s: California becomes a medium-tax state, and budget pressures become acute.

The full impact of California's tax revolt on the State's finances can best be seen from a long-term perspective. On a per capita basis, California's total state and local tax burden ranked an average of fourth nationally during the 1970s. That average dropped to ninth during the 1980s and 17th in 1993-94. On a percentage-of-income basis, the decline was more dramatic. California's national rank during most of the 1970s was fifth, falling to 20th during the 1980s and 34th in 1993-94.[9] Clearly, the State could no longer support public spending at the high level possible before Proposition 13 passed in 1978. The demand for public services, however, did not decline correspondingly, leaving the State with a constant budgetary tug-of-war between programs competing for a share of the tax base.

The pressure of such competing demands became particularly difficult during recessionary periods such as the early 1990s, when revenue turned down but spending pressures increased. The slowdown in economic activity that accompanies a recession has a negative impact upon all revenue sources, especially sales tax receipts, the most volatile element in the State's tax base. (See Table 3.)

---

[7] California Constitution, Article XIII-A, Sections 3-4. The great majority of other states require only a simple majority vote of the Legislature to pass a tax increase. (See Appendix A.)

[8] California Constitution, Article XIII-B; Revenue & Taxation Code, Section 17041. A majority of other states have some type of spending limitation. (See Appendix B.) It should be noted that State spending has not been significantly limited by Article XIII-B for more than a decade. The Governor's proposed budget for the current fiscal year, for example, was more than $8 billion under the spending limit. (*Governor's Budget Summary 1997-98*, Schedule 12-A, page A-54.)

[9] See Tables 41 and 45 in the Economic Report of the Governor 1997, pages A-30-31. On the Department of Finance website (http://www.dof.ca.gov) bunder Financial and Economic Data.

On the expenditure side, outlays for public health and social service entitlement programs are at their highest level during recessionary periods. (See the Health and Social Services sections of Part II below.)

Such conflicting pressures were felt most acutely in the struggle over the 1991-92 budget when, in the depths of a recession, the State faced a potential deficit of $14 billion. To limit the deficit, the Legislature and the Governor agreed to a three-part package with tax increases of $7 billion, program cuts of $3.5 billion and a large amount of spending deferrals/revenue accelerations and cost shifts to the federal and local governments. The projected deficit for the following fiscal year (1992-93) was more than $10 billion. Program reductions and cost deferrals, but not revenue increases, again comprised a major part of the response from the Governor and the Legislature. Political rancor delayed adoption of the 1992-93 budget until a record 63 days after the new fiscal year had begun.

Current Outlook: Out of recession, but caution still called for

The intense focus on California's budgetary problems arising from the recession of the early 1990s has subsided during the past three fiscal years. Economic recovery put unexpected additional revenues into the State's coffers and enabled the elimination of the deficit built up during the recession.

At the close of the 1997 session of the Legislature, tax reductions exceeding $1 billion, as well as major new spending obligations, were enacted. These measures began to take effect in the 1997-98 fiscal year, with full implementation in the following two fiscal years.[10] The underlying assumption is that economic growth will be sufficient to finance the higher expenditures, even with reductions in the revenue base. The Legislative Analyst's long-term budget outlook published in December 1997 predicts that the State will be able to accommodate these new commitments through the turn of the century, based primarily on an expectation of continued healthy economic growth and declining human services caseloads.[11]

Although it appears that the budgetary imbalance which plagued the State during the early 1990s has been eliminated, continual vigilance and a long-term perspective are essential to prevent problems in the future, especially in times of economic distress. As past history has so clearly demonstrated, it is difficult, if not impossible, to predict how long the State's current spending and revenue levels will remain in relative balance. Budget makers need to guard against the temptation to expand spending commitments during economic upswings beyond the level that can be sustained without unpopular tax increases when the economy slows or declines.

The Governor and the Legislature will need to keep these considerations in mind as they develop budget policies and priorities for the 21ˢᵗ century.

---

[10] *Governor's Budget Summary 1997-98*, page 63.
[11] Legislative Analyst's Office, *California's Fiscal Outlook* (Nov. 1997).

Where the Money Comes From

An overview of California's revenue sources

The revenues available to support state government and its many and varied programs consist primarily of the proceeds from three taxes: the sales tax, the personal income tax, and the bank and corporation tax (the business income tax).[12] These three taxes produce nearly all the revenue for the State's General Fund, which in turn provides major support for programs controlled through the state budget process (subject to constitutional and statutory limits). State revenues also include bond proceeds and special funds containing moneys received from taxes, such as the gas tax, earmarked for specified purposes. In addition to revenue generated directly by the State, large amounts of money are received from the federal government and used to support a variety of specific programs.

Most state revenue goes to programs administered at the local level (e.g., K-12 education by school districts and various health and social welfare programs by counties). Most of these programs also receive local contributions, still substantially derived from property taxes, in addition to state and federal subventions. (Local contributions, amounting to $9 billion in the case of school support, are not included in the Budget Act.)

Table 1 shows the estimated composition of state revenues for the current year.

Table 1:
Major State Taxes and License Fees, 1997-98 (in millions)

Revenue Source	General Fund	Special Funds
Personal Income Tax	$25,980	
Sales and Use Taxes	17,545	1,974
Bank and Corporation Tax	5,835	
Motor Vehicle Fees	36	5,401
Highway Users Taxes		2,907
Insurance Tax	1,224	
Estate and Gift Taxes	731	
Liquor Taxes and Fees	270	
Tobacco Taxes	165	486
Horse Racing Licenses	44	37
Total	**$51,830**	**$10,805**

Source: Governor's Budget Summary, 1998-99

---

[12] Revenue & Taxation Code, Division II, Parts 1, 10 and 11.

Components of General Fund revenues

The General Fund is the principal operating fund for the majority of state governmental activities and is the depository for most of the State's major revenue sources. It consists of revenues not required by law to be credited to any other fund, as well as earnings from the investment of state moneys not allocable to other funds.

Taxes on personal income and retail sales are the State's major sources of General Fund revenues. These two revenue sources are sensitive to changes in the State's economy. Collections fell sharply in the early 1990s recession, but have recovered with the recent improvement in the State's economy. The two next largest revenue sources are the bank and corporation tax and the insurance tax.

Personal income tax

The personal income tax is the General Fund's largest single revenue source, accounting for 49% of total receipts in 1997-98. As set forth in Table 2, California's personal income tax is one of the most progressive in the nation, with the top 5% of taxpayers contributing more than 50% of the tax paid. In 1993-94, California ranked 12th nationally in per capita income taxes and 18ᵗʰ on percentage of income.[13]

Table 2:
Percentage of Income Tax Revenues Collected by Income Level

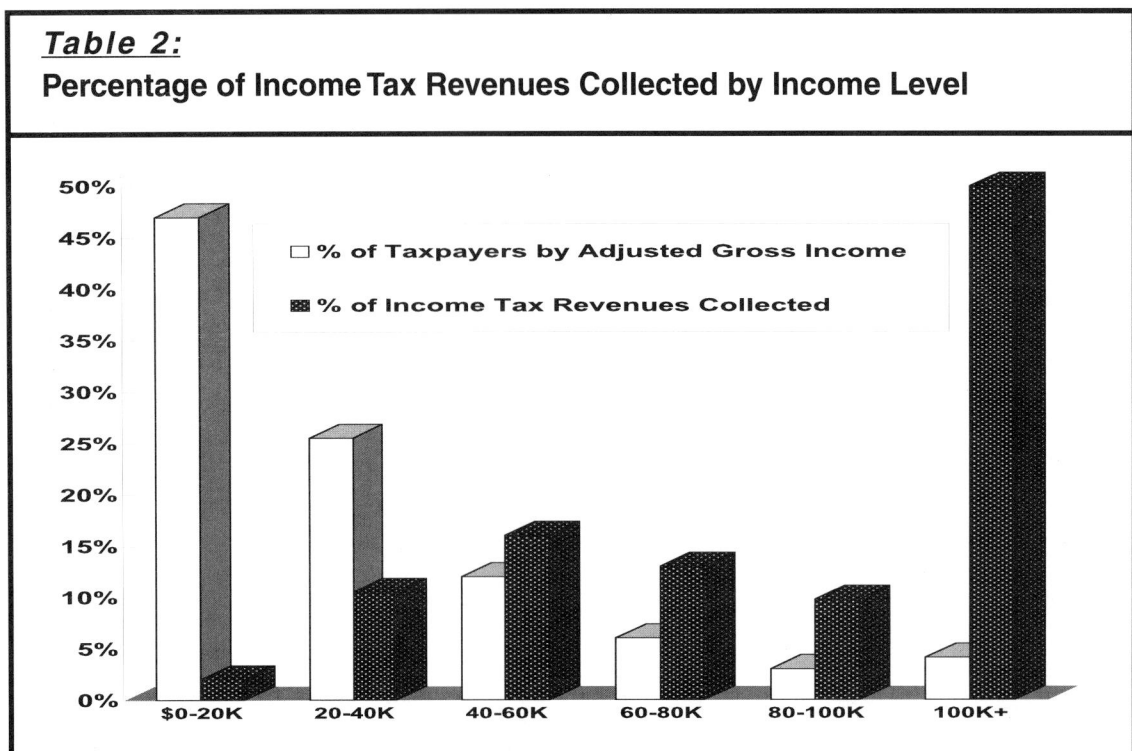

□ % of Taxpayers by Adjusted Gross Income

▨ % of Income Tax Revenues Collected

Source: Governor's Budget Summary, 1994-1995

---

[13] *Economic Report of the Governor 1997*, Tables 42 and 46, pages A-30-31; Tables 57 and 58, page A-37.

Sales and use tax

The sales and use tax is the second largest source of General Fund revenue—and its most volatile (see Table 3)—accounting for about 34% of collections in 1997-98. The tax is levied on the sale of tangible personal property to the ultimate consumer, including both individuals and businesses. The major categories of property exempt from sales tax are food for home consumption, prescription drugs, natural gas and piped water. The sales tax does not apply to personal or business services or to intangible assets (i.e., stocks, bonds, bank accounts and intellectual property such as patents, copyrights and trademarks).

Table 3:
The Volatility of Sales Tax Revenues

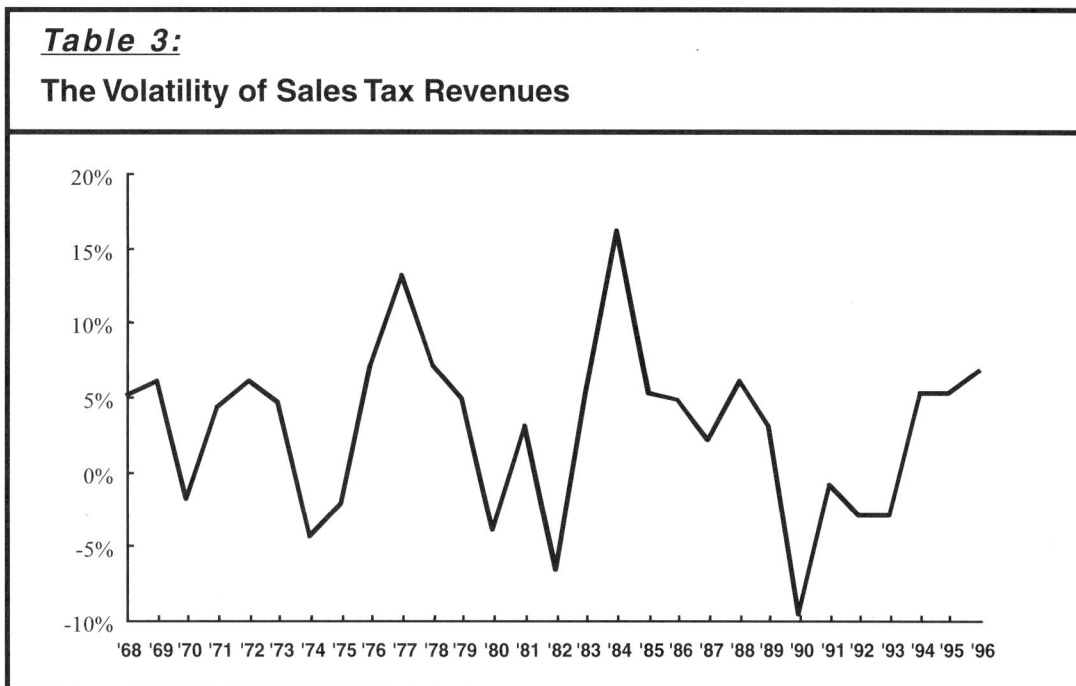

Source: Governor's Budget Summary, 1997-1998

The sales tax has several components. First, a general 5% rate generates revenue for the General Fund. Add to that 0.5% for counties to provide indigent health and related services and another 0.5% for city and county public safety activities, which brings the overall state sales tax rate to 6%. Additional local rates begin at 1.25% and can go as high as 2.75%, creating a minimum total sales and use tax of 7.25% and a maximum of 8.75%. On top of all that, counties are authorized to increase the rate by 0.5% for specified purposes with voter approval.

In 1993-94, California ranked 11th in the nation in per capita sales taxes paid, and 17th on a percentage-of-income basis.[14]

---

[14] *Ibid.,* Tables 57 and 58, pages A-37.

Bank and corporation tax

The bank and corporation tax (business income tax) is California's third-largest source of General Fund revenues, accounting for 12% of total receipts. An 8.84% rate is applied to corporate profits, and banks pay an additional 2% tax on their net income in lieu of personal property and business license taxes. In 1993-94, California was at the top level among the states in business income taxes, ranking seventh on a per capita basis and eighth as a percentage of income.[15]

Revenues for special purposes

Through legislation and ballot measures, California has created more than 300 separate special funds with unique financing mechanisms, revenue sources and appropriation authorities. By far the largest special fund spending authority is the California Transportation Commission, with jurisdiction over the multi-billion-dollar revenue flow from the State's gas tax and other motor vehicle-related sources. The proceeds of those tax revenues are restricted by laws dictating the support of particular functions or activities of government. The funds included in those classifications are expended primarily for transportation, law enforcement, capital outlay, and the regulation of businesses, professions and vocations. Motor vehicle-related taxes and fees account for about 60% of all special fund revenue.

In general, special fund revenues consist of three categories of income: (1) receipts from tax levies allocated to specified functions, such as motor vehicle taxes and fees; (2) charges for special services, including business and professional license fees; and (3) rental royalties and other receipts designated for particular purposes, such as oil and gas royalties allocated to capital outlay activities (although such royalties can be, and often are, used for General Fund purposes as well).

As set forth in Table 7, California's special funds totaled about $14 billion in 1997-98, accounting for approximately 21% of total state revenue (excluding federal funds).

Such dedicated or "earmarked" taxes have become increasingly popular as public skepticism over executive and legislative budget decision-making has risen to new heights. Apparently the public prefers to pay taxes earmarked for favored specific purposes, rather than allow the Legislature and the governor to allocate all tax revenues. Examples of that public preference are the passage in recent years of several "ballot-box budgeting" initiatives—such as the 1988 Proposition 99 increase in cigarette taxes of 25 cents to finance a variety of health and environmental programs (including, in particular, anti-smoking programs) and the 1993 Proposition 172 half-cent sales tax increase to fund law enforcement.

---

[15] Stephen Kroes, *Taxing California: Analysis of 1993-94 Federal, State and Local Tax Burdens,* Cal-Tax Digest (September 1997), pages 12-14.

As shown in Table 4, General Fund revenue growth during the recession of the early 1990s was anemic compared to the growth in special funds. Between fiscal years 1988-89 and 1993-94, General Fund revenues increased just 8.5% while special funds grew by 93%.[16] The disparity was due to the much greater volatility of General Fund tax sources. Since the end of the recession, however, the reverse has been true: General Fund revenues have grown faster than special fund revenues.

Table 4:

Growth in the General and Special Funds, 1987-98
(in billions)

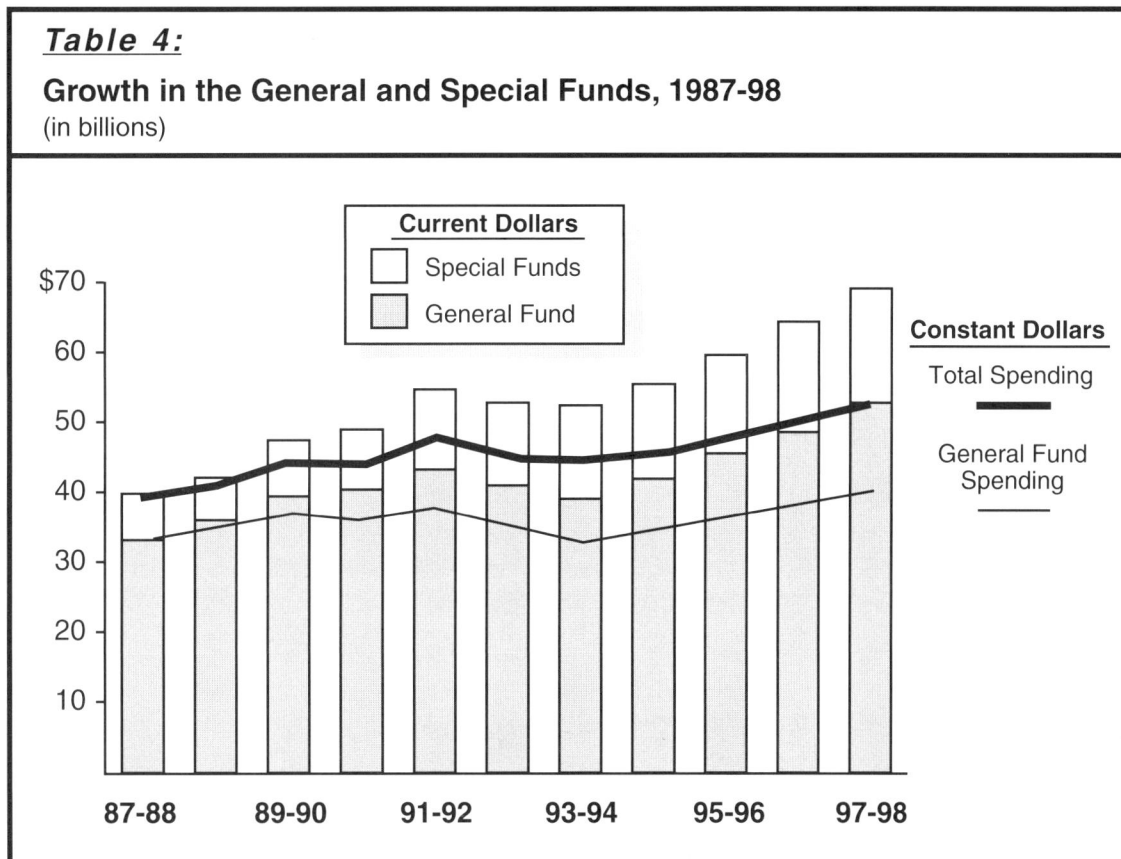

Source: California Spending Plan 1997-98, Legislative Analyst's Office

Bond Funds

Many of the State's capital outlay projects are funded with borrowed money. That borrowing takes two forms. First, **general obligation bonds** are issued with voter approval for specific purposes, such as construction of local schools and state prisons, and state park acquisition and development. These bonds carry the full faith and credit of the State, which minimizes borrowing costs. Between 1980 and 1996, the voters authorized the issuance of more than $27 billion in general obligation bonds to fund capital projects.[17]

---

[16] Department of Finance historical data in Schedule 6 of the *Governor's Budget Summary 1997-98*, page A-19.
[17] *Governor's Budget Summary 1997-98*, Schedule 11, pages A-52-53 *(excluding self-liquidating issues)*.

The second type of borrowing involves the issuance of **lease payment (lease-revenue) bonds.** These debt instruments do not require voter approval and are paid off by annual lease payments for the facilities financed by the bonds. The appropriations for the lease payments come directly out of the budgets of the agencies that use the facilities. Without full faith and credit status, lease-revenue bonds carry interest rates approximately one-half percent higher than the State's general obligation bonds. Lease-revenue bond issues generally cost 15% to 20% more than equivalent general-obligation issues (7% to 10% when adjusted for inflation).[18] The lease-revenue bonds issued through 1997 totaled approximately $6.5 billion.

Efforts by the Department of Corrections to build more prisons in the early 1990s provide a prime example of why and how lease-revenue financing occurs. When the voters did not approve bond issues for the construction of new prisons in 1990 and 1992, the Department requested legislation authorizing the sale of lease-revenue bonds. The legislation was approved, the bonds were sold, and the prisons were built without the specific voter approval that was previously sought but denied.

Federal subventions

Comparable to the amount of revenues generated by the state sales tax, federal subventions (financial support) serve as a major provider of funding for state programs. Table 10 shows the composition of the more than $32 billion in federal subventions included in the State's 1997-98 budget.[19]

Where the Money Goes

State spending in California has been growing constantly since the end of World War II—more slowly during times of recession and more vigorously in times of economic expansion. Since 1980, in spite of two recessions, state spending has grown at an average annual rate of more than 5%.[20]

---

[18] Legislative Analyst's Office, *Uses and Costs of Lease-Payment Bonds* (May 3, 1995).

[19] In the past, federal subventions have been a highly variable source of revenue for state programs. Between 1990 and 1993, for example, federal spending in California increased by almost 48%. *(Briffault, Balancing Acts—The Reality Behind State Balanced Budget Requirements,* Twentieth Century Fund (1996), pages 28-29. At present, a downward trend seems more likely as Congress and the President seek to balance the federal budget and return more control and fiscal responsibility to the states.

[20] *Governor's Budget Summary 1997-98,* Schedule 6, page A-19.

Breakdown of state appropriations

California's state budget takes several forms in the course of the budget process. The Governor's Budget is an inches-thick document containing the Governor's spending proposals for the coming fiscal year, primarily for ongoing programs pursuant to existing state law. It also contains spending schedules, program descriptions and objectives, multi-year program costs, and various budget adjustments. The budget bill, prepared by the Department of Finance and submitted to the Legislature in January along with the Governor's Budget, contains actual provisions for appropriation items and "control language."[21] The budget bill is introduced as proposed legislation and becomes the Budget Act after being modified and passed by the Legislature and then signed into law by the Governor.

Total state spending in the 1997-98 Budget Act includes appropriations from the General Fund, special funds, bond funds and federal funds as shown in Table 5.

Table 5:
1997-1998 Total Spending
(in billions)

General Fund	52.8
Special Funds	14.4
Bond Funds	2.1
Federal Funds*	32.6
Total	**$101.9**

* Per Governor's January Proposed Budget
Source: 1997-98 Final Budget, Department of Finance

Less than 20% of the budget is spent directly by state agencies, and most of that money is spent on higher education and the prison system. The bulk of state revenue is actually spent by local governmental entities such as school districts, counties and cities. School districts are supported primarily by subventions received from the State, and counties act as agents of the State in administering the principal share of many programs at the local level, including health and social welfare programs and the court system.

Not all revenues spent on state programs are included in the state budget. While federal subventions are shown within the recipient department's budget, not all federal funds used to support state programs in California are reflected in the Budget Act. Local contributions to programs funded jointly by state and local government are also excluded from the Budget Act, as are retirement funds and state public enterprise funds (such as bridge tolls), state investment funds and private funds left in trust to the State.

The General Fund–Allocating resources among competing demands

The General Fund is the State's main operating fund. Money from the General Fund supports such programs as primary, secondary and community college

---

[21] "Control language" is contained in the concluding sections of the Budget Act. Those sections "generally provide additional authorizations or place additional restrictions on one or more of the itemized appropriations contained" in the earlier appropriations section. *(Governor's Budget Summary 1997-98, page A-3.)* For example, the Legislature might attach to an appropriation for a particular program a requirement that a study be done of the effectiveness of the program and the results be reported to the Legislature.

education; the University of California and the California State University systems; prisons and the criminal justice system; and various health and social welfare services. The breakdown of the $52.8 billion of 1997-98 General Fund expenditures is set forth in Table 6.

Table 6:

Composition of the General Fund, 1997-98
(in billions)

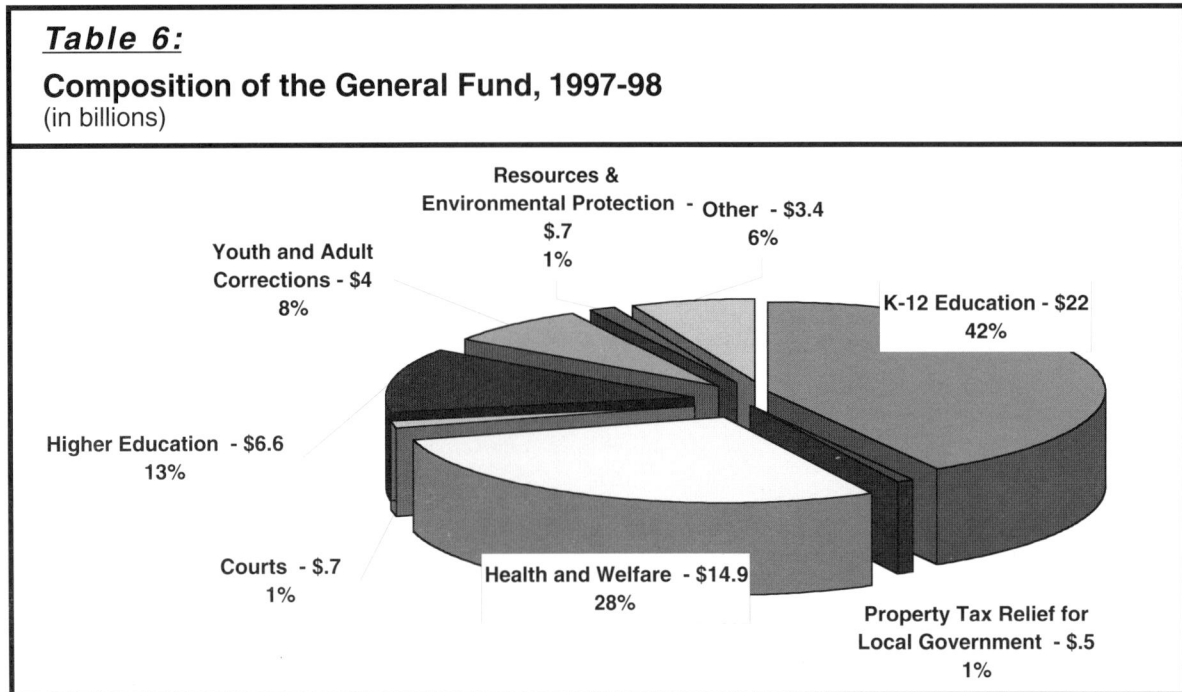

Resources & Environmental Protection - $.7 — 1%
Other - $3.4 — 6%
Youth and Adult Corrections - $4 — 8%
K-12 Education - $22 — 42%
Higher Education - $6.6 — 13%
Courts - $.7 — 1%
Health and Welfare - $14.9 — 28%
Property Tax Relief for Local Government - $.5 — 1%

Source: 1997-98 Final Budget, Department of Finance

The General Fund is not the only source of revenue for many of those programs. For example, as indicated above, K-12 Education receives funds from both the federal government and local property taxes. Several major health and social welfare programs are funded jointly with the federal government.

Theoretically, the General Fund is distinguished from other funds in that state policy-makers have discretion over how to allocate General Fund dollars. Expenditures from special funds and bond funds, in contrast, are normally dedicated to specified purposes. However, in recent years, constitutional and statutory restrictions have dramatically reduced the Legislature's General Fund expenditure authority, particularly with respect to schools.[22]

Special Funds–Earmarked financing for favored programs

Constitutional provisions, statutory initiatives or ordinary statutes govern most spending from the State's 300-plus special funds. Although most special funds are reviewed as part of the normal budget process, their dedication to specific purposes limits the flexibility of the Legislature and the Governor in establishing the State's

---

[22] See Appendix B of the Commission's Preliminary Report for a compendium of some of the major restraints on the fiscal powers of the Legislature.

budget priorities. Constitutional special fund provisions are binding on the Legislature and may be changed only by a vote of the people. In cases where the voters have established financing for a program through the initiative process, those funds generally cannot be used to sustain other programs that may, in fact, have a higher public priority. In most other cases, a statute must be amended or suspended to allow special funds to be redirected for purposes other than those specified. As a consequence, powerful interest groups have often sponsored initiatives or persuaded the Legislature to enact special funds or budgeting procedures that protect their favored programs from budget cuts or loss of tax preferences.

Table 7:	
Composition of Special Funds, 1997-98 (in millions)	
Education	$53
Health and Welfare	3,369
Higher Education	667
Business Transportation and Housing	4,191
Local Government Subventions	3,622
Resources	898
Environmental Protection	545
State and Consumer Services	394
Trade and Commerce	15
Youth and Adult Corrections	10
Other	658
Total	**$14,422**

Source: 1997-98 Final Budget, Department of Finance

Funding state programs through the budget process can involve interplay among the various types of funds. For example, although the courts have placed limits on the practice,[23] lawmakers have sometimes transferred resources from special funds to supplement insufficient revenue in the General Fund to maintain desired spending during times of fiscal distress.[24]

Special fund protections include:

Constitutional protection: Motor vehicle fuel taxes may be used only for construction and maintenance of "public streets and highways" and construction of "mass transit guide ways." (State Constitution, Article XIX, Section 1)

Initiative statute: A major portion of the state cigarette tax is levied and allocated for health and environmental services pursuant to a 1988 voter-approved initiative.

---

[23] See, for example, *American Lung Association, et al v. Wilson,* 51 Cal. App. 4th 743 (1996) (Proposition 99 case) and *Malibu Video Systems v. Brown* (L.A. Sup Ct. No. BC 101-796), Judgment filed Feb. 14, 1996 (regulatory special fund cases).

[24] See, for example, the Budget Act of 1991-92 (Chapter 118, Statures of 1991). One of the "control sections" of that Act, Section 11.50(d), transferred to the General Fund $80 million of tidelands oil revenue from the purposes set forth in Public Resources Code Section 6217. Similar transfers were made by the Budget Acts of the following two fiscal years. In this situation, the transferred funds had only statutory protection and could, therefore, be transferred by a simple legislative action (the Budget Act).

Statute: Revenues from leases of state lands are placed in a special fund for allocation to specific activities, although that statute is frequently amended or suspended and the money appropriated for other purposes.[25]

The size and scope of the State's special fund programs are summarized in Table 7.

Bond Funds – Primarily spent for long-term investment

The 1997-98 budget allocated approximately $800 million—slightly more than 1% of total spending—to capital outlay activities. Although the executive branch sends an annual capital outlay report to the Legislature,[26] there is no statutory or budgeting system for the development and financing of the State's long-term capital needs. The current system of capital outlay budgeting is ad hoc and changes from year to year depending upon legislative and executive priorities.

Table 8:
Uses of Bond Funds, 1997-98
(in millions)

Education (K-12)	135
Higher Education	544
Transportation	1,014
Youth and Adult Corrections	21
Resources	260
Environmental Protection	93
State and Consumer	62
Total	**$2,130**

Source: 1997-98 Final Budget, Department of Finance

The amount of state bond funds used to meet local capital outlay needs is very substantial. Since the early 1980s, the State has used its long-term financing capacity to pay for the construction of local K-12 schools. Of approximately $36 billion in voter-approved general obligation bonds issued since 1980, almost $9.9 billion—or about 30%—has been allocated to local school construction.

The expected uses of bond proceeds in the current fiscal year are set forth in Table 8. Table 9 summarizes the use of bond funds since 1980.

Federal funds—Federal money for state programs

Federal funds are moneys transferred to the State for specific purposes as provided in federal law. Only those federal subventions linked to specific state expenditures are itemized in the Budget Act. Social welfare and health programs, such as Medi-Cal, receive two-thirds of all federal funds. With the passage of the federal Personal Responsibility and Work Opportunity Reconciliation Act of 1996 (also known as the Welfare Reform Act), the level of state responsibility for the expenditure and administration of federal welfare appropriations was dramatically increased. Education, highway, criminal justice and housing programs, in particular, also receive substantial federal funding. Future "devolution" efforts similar to the Welfare Reform Act could affect some of those programs as well.

---

[25] See, for example, the sections of the Budget Acts of 1991-92, 1992-93 & 1993-94 discussed in the preceding footnote.

[26] See, for example, Department of Finance, Annual Capital Outlay Report for 1997-98.

Table 9: Uses of Bond Funds, 1980-98 (in millions)		
Activity	**Amount Borrowed**	
	General Obligation	Lease-Revenue
Education (K-12)	9,890	
Higher Education	3,640	2,411
Transportation	5,000	
Youth and Adult Corrections	4,087	3,112
Resources	4,686	
Environmental Protection	440	
Housing	605	
Health and Welfare	150	
State buildings and facilities		991
Other	760	
Self-Liquidating (Veterans housing, harbor and water resources)	7,020	
Total	**$36,278**	**$6,514**

Source: 1997-98 Governor's Budget Summary, Schedule 11

The uses currently being made of federal subventions are set forth in Table 10.

Table 10: Uses of Federal Funds, 1997-98 (in millions)	
Education (K-12)	3,173
Higher Education	4,108
Health and Welfare	21,637
Business Transportation and Housing	1,916
Trade and Commerce	7
Youth and Adult Corrections	389
Resources and Environmental Protection	156
General Government	746
Other	477
Total	**$32,609**

Source: Governor's 1997-98 January Budget Estimate

Major General Fund expenditure categories

The General Fund contains the vast majority of state spending subject to annual legislative review. More than 90% of the General Fund is consumed by five major programs: K-12 education, health, social welfare, corrections and higher education.

K-12 education and community colleges

By far the largest appropriations in the state budget are for K-12 education programs and community colleges. The proposed 1997-98 funding for these programs is $22 billion—more than 41% of projected General Fund expenditures. The State expects that an additional $10 billion in funding for education will come from local property taxes.[27] These moneys are actually spent by local school districts, subject to the statutory requirements of the state Education Code.

For most of the 1990s, per-pupil spending for K-12 education grew by slightly more than 1% annually. Per-pupil spending for 1997-98, however, grew by almost 8% over the 1996-97 average, to a total of $5,144.[28]

Since the passage of Proposition 98 in 1988, school and community college funding levels have been established by constitutionally mandated formulas. These complex formulas have created numerous controversies about funding calculations of the required by Proposition 98, particularly during the early 1990s recession when the State's revenues dropped substantially below forecasts. Funding problems will also be created by the rapidly increasing student population that will require a considerable escalation in spending levels over the next quarter-century.

Health

Health programs in California are financed by a combination of federal, state and county dollars. Again, complex formulas dictate the distribution of these funds. In 1997-98, Medi-Cal—the State's Medicaid program for low-income residents—will account for more than 90% of state health spending. Like K-12 education, Medi-Cal is administered locally (by the counties), although the great majority of the funding comes from state and federal subventions.

When Congress passed the Medicaid law in 1965 creating state health-care financing programs for the poor and disabled in conjunction with the federal government, states assumed greater financial burdens than they expected. During its first decade, Medicaid expenditures grew at an annual rate in excess of 25%, and for the next seven years at a rate of almost 17%. Slowing during the 1980s, the rate of increase rose again during the recession of the early 1990s.[29]

---

[27] Legislative Analyst's Office, *California Spending Plan 1997-98* (October, 1997), page 28.

[28] *Ibid.*, page 27. It should be noted that National Education Association figures for 1994-95 show California's per-pupil spending for that year ($4,731) more than $1,000 below the national average ($5,907), placing the State 37ᵗʰ in per-pupil spending among all the states. (Governor's Proposed Budget 1994-95, page 25.) The State's increases in education spending since that time still leave California far below national average per-pupil spending.

[29] Center for the Study of the States, State Fiscal Brief No. 47 (January 1998), page 5.

The number of people eligible for Medi-Cal grew from 11% of the general population in the late 1980s to more than 17% in 1994-95, at the recessionary peak.[30] Expenditures for Medi-Cal in California have grown by 60% since 1991. The 1997-98 General Fund budget includes $7 billion for Medi-Cal, 13.7% of the General Fund budget and an amount second only to funding for K-12 education.[31]

Social services

Historically, California's largest social welfare program was the Aid to Families with Dependent Children (AFDC). During the mid-1980s, a time of economic prosperity, California's AFDC costs increased by less than 2% annually. In contrast, the State's 1992-93 AFDC costs increased 7%. Highly correlated to the economy, the 1992 rise in the AFDC caseload was a reflection of the State's severe recession. In 1995-96, as the California economy began to recover from the recession, AFDC spending declined.[32]

In August 1996, Congress passed historic federal welfare reform legislation, repealing the AFDC entitlement program and creating a new block grant program called Temporary Assistance for Needy Families (TANF). TANF places a cap on the number of years welfare recipients may receive assistance and institutes federal block grants to states for welfare programs. The overall impact of those changes is yet to be determined, but promises to be substantial.

The State's other large social welfare entitlement program is the Supplemental Security Income/State Supplemental Payment (SSI/SSP) program, which provides income support for aged, blind and disabled low-income individuals. Although the federal government pays all of the SSI cash grants, states have the option of supplementing that assistance. Most states do not offer additional monetary support. In contrast, California provides supplements in the form of SSP grants for which the total proposed appropriation in 1997-98 is $1.7 billion.[33] As in the case of TANF, the number of individuals in California receiving SSI/SSP will change, with corresponding budget implications, as a result of the recent major changes in federal and state welfare laws.

Youth and adult corrections

During the past two decades, spending by the State of California to incarcerate criminals has grown at nearly double the rate for any other General Fund program. Spending for state-run correctional facilities increased twelvefold between fiscal years 1976-77 and 1996-97, more than three times the increase in total General Fund spending.[34] The 1997-98 corrections budget of $4.3 billion is approximately $423 million more than the previous year's appropriation—an 11% increase. Although

[30] Historical caseload data from *Governor's Budget Summaries, 1995-96*, page 159; 1998-99, page 117.
[31] *Governor's Budget Summary 1997-98*, page 105.
[32] *Ibid.*, pages 98-99; historical data from previous Governor's Budget Summaries.
[33] *Ibid.*, page 102.
[34] Charts C and C-1 in the Background Information provided with the Governor's proposed 1998-99 budget. Available on the Department of Finance website at http://www.dof.ca.gov/html/bud_docs/charts (from the DOF home page, click on California Budget, then FAQs, then Background Information).

youth and adult corrections will probably continue to claim a growing share of the State's resources, the growth rate, even with the "three strikes" initiative in full operation, has not been as high as earlier feared. The Legislative Analyst forecasts that corrections expenditures will increase at an average annual rate of about 6.1% through the year 2000.[35]

Higher education

California's Master Plan for Higher Education has long been viewed as a model in the nation. It establishes a broad range of goals and responsibilities among locally run two-year community colleges, the California State University and University of California systems, and private colleges and universities. The State's overarching goal has been to provide low-cost access to high-quality institutions of higher education for all qualified Californians.

In recent years, General Fund spending for higher education has grown more slowly than other state programs, such as health, social services and corrections. In 1980-81, spending for higher education accounted for 15.6% of General Fund spending. By 1996-97, that amount had dropped to 12%. The full impact of the relative decline in the level of State support has been offset considerably by substantial increases in student fees.[36]

Sharp cuts in support for higher education during economic downturns has called into question the viability of the Master Plan. As demands for access to quality higher education increase, with an expected 30% growth in the college-age population over the next decade, the Governor and Legislature will face heightened pressure to examine long-range fiscal and program planning. Although the community colleges are covered by Proposition 98's revenue guarantee, the rest of higher education is not. After the close of the 1997 session of the Legislature, the Governor vetoed legislation which would have enacted a guaranteed level of spending for the public universities.[37]

Other General Fund spending

After the Big Five, the next largest General Fund expenditure category is debt service. The 1997-98 budget includes approximately $2 billion for debt service on general obligation bonds. The remaining 5% of the General Fund is spent on a variety of state programs, including resources and environmental protection which consume some $700 million (1.4%) of the General Fund.

---

[35] Legislative Analyst's Office, *California Fiscal Outlook* (November 1997), page 22. Due to an expected decrease in federal funding, however, the Analyst estimates that the State's General Fund corrections expenditures for the period will increase by 9% annually.
[36] For a full discussion of the fiscal pressures facing the State's public higher education system, see *A State of Learning: California and the Dream Higher Education in the 21ˢᵗ Century,* California Citizens Commission on Higher Education (June 1998).
[37] A. B. 1415 (Bustamante), 1997-98 Session.

Tax Expenditures

There is an important aspect of the State's tax base which, although part of the revenue structure, is similar in its economic impact to special fund expenditures. Tax expenditures, created by elected officials to encourage certain taxpayer activities, are defined by the Legislative Analyst as "the various tax exclusions, exceptions, preferential tax rates, credits and deferrals which reduce the amount of revenue collected from the State's basic tax structure." While no money is actually spent, these preferences are considered expenditures because "the benefits they provide to individuals and businesses make them very much like regular direct governmental expenditures, except that they are paid for by reduced tax collections rather than through the normal legislative appropriation process."[38]

Table 11: Tax Expenditures Enacted Since 1990 (annual loss in millions)	
Personal Income Tax	
Stay-at-home parent credit	25
Extension of net operating loss carryover	45
Establish Los Angeles revitalization zone	7
Manufacturer's investment credit	32
Limited partnership source rule	10
Total	**119**
Sales and Use Tax	
Free newspapers and periodicals	20
Subscription periodicals	10
Watercraft common carrier fuel	21
Manufacturing equipment for start-up firms	10
Total	**61**
Bank and Corporations Tax	
Extension of net operating loss carryover	164
Extension of research/ development credit	86
Manufacturer's investment credit	365
Expanded credit union income exemption	13
Total	**628**
Total	**$808**

Source: Tax Expenditure Report 1997-98
Department of Finance

Table 11 lists examples of tax expenditures enacted by the Legislature during the 1990s, despite the financial pressures during that time.

Major differences between how tax expenditures are created and how they are eliminated gives them an important place in California's fiscal system. There was a time when it was relatively simple to make changes in the State's taxation system: the same number of "aye" votes were required to increase or decrease a tax. For the most part, such changes were achieved through a simple majority vote of the Legislature. As a result, the State could balance equity and efficiency in the tax structure with identical vote requirements. For example, the State might increase the sales tax rate in order to finance a concurrent reduction in the property tax by the same legislative vote.

With the voters' enactment of Proposition 13 in 1978, the tax

---

[38] Legislative Analyst's Office, *Analysis of the 1991-92 Tax Expenditure Budget* (May 1991), page 3.

system changed fundamentally. This constitutional measure requires a two-thirds majority vote for "any changes in state taxes enacted for the purposes of increasing revenues... whether by increased rates or changes in methods of computation."[39] Under this Prop. 13 provision, a simple majority vote may still enact a tax expenditure, but a two-thirds vote is required to remove the same provision. As a result, it has become much more difficult to reduce or eliminate tax expenditures.

Table 12: Estimated Annual Revenue Loss From Tax Expenditures (in billions)	
Personal Income Tax	13.0
Sales and Use Tax	1.0
Bank and Corporations Tax	3.0
Other	.5
Total	**$17.5**

Source: Tax Expenditure Report 1997-98
Department of Finance

The Department of Finance annually estimates the amount of revenue lost to tax preferences. DOF's annual Tax Expenditure Report for 1997-98 estimates tax expenditure losses equal to about 33% of total General Fund revenue. Local government resources are greatly affected by the revenue lost to exemptions from sales and use taxes, since about one-third of sales tax revenue pays for city and county services.

The Budget Process – Making It All Fit

The state budget process is the State's method for allocating revenue, within constitutional and statutory constraints, thus resolving the pressures and conflicts that inevitably arise in an enterprise as large and complex as California's state government. The Governor and the 120-member Legislature have the annual responsibility of directing how a huge amount of the public's money (estimated to exceed $75 billion in the 1998-99 fiscal year) is to be spent, and in the process determining how state and local government in California will function. How well they fulfill this responsibility has an impact upon the lives of all Californians, although very few citizens have even a rudimentary understanding of how elected officials accomplish this task.

Stages of the State budget process

The state budget operates on a July 1 through June 30 fiscal year, as do almost all other states. Although the 1997-98 fiscal year started July 1, spending authority for many state programs did not begin until August 18, 1997, when the Governor signed the budget. In general, the time frame to develop and pass a budget spans at least 18 months, with the last eight months of that process involving the most intense decision-making on the part of elected officials.

---

[39] California Constitution, Article XIII A, Section 3.

The budget proceeds in the following three major stages.

Executive branch development—creating a spending plan

Budget preparation begins with state agencies developing proposals and schedules for review by the Department of Finance (DOF). The Director of Finance issues guidelines for budget preparation to departments as much as 18 months before the beginning of a fiscal year. This document provides assumptions about General Fund revenues, caseload growth patterns and the Governor's stated budget priorities. For example, departments might be told to submit a budget with spending reduced by 5% in a year when slower revenue growth requires a reduction in overall state spending or when other programs require increased funding.

The DOF, in turn, estimates revenues and develops final budget proposals and schedules after making adjustments to reflect the Governor's priorities. This is generally done in the fall, more than six months before the fiscal year begins on July 1.

The Governor may submit revised budget proposals at any time during the Legislature's budget deliberations. A major revision is typically done in late May, after income and property tax receipts are tallied in April. Revenue and expenditure estimates, upon which the proposed budget is based, are six months old, and the estimates upon which the current budget was based are more than a year old. In a state as large and diverse as California, accurate budget estimates are exceedingly difficult, if not impossible, to achieve that far in advance.

Legislative review and approval—taking the plan apart and putting it back together

Upon presentation of the Governor's budget in January, the budget committee chairs in both houses of the Legislature introduce identical budget bills reflecting the Governor's proposals. This is the only point at which there is a constitutional requirement that the budget must be balanced. From that point until the Legislature sends a budget back to the Governor for signature, the Legislature has control of the budget and may substitute its priorities for the Governor's. The Legislative Analyst's Office provides the Legislature with an analysis of the budget along with recommendations.

Budget committees in each house consider the Analyst's recommendations as they review the Governor's budget proposals. Each budget committee is divided into subject matter subcommittees that hold public budget hearings from mid-March to mid-May. By that time, the two bills are usually very different, having been amended to reflect the priorities of each house. After the April tax receipts are tallied, the Governor generally submits the "May Revision" to the original proposed budget. These revised budget proposals become part of the final legislative budget deliberations.

After each house passes its version of the budget, a budget conference committee resolves the differences and creates one final budget bill. Historically, the conference committee has been a three-way discussion involving the two houses of the Legislature and the Governor, represented by the DOF. However, in recent years the conference committee process has been superseded by the "Big Five" (the Governor, the President Pro Tem of the Senate, the Speaker of the Assembly, and the minority party leaders of both houses), who meet in private to negotiate the final budget. The outcome of their deliberations is incorporated into the conference committee report to both houses.

The resulting budget bill is then voted upon by each house (passage requires a two-thirds vote of the membership), and the bill is sent to the Governor. The Constitution requires final passage of the budget by June 15 of each year;[40] however, the Legislature has sent a budget to the Governor on time in only three of the last 10 years.

The legislative calendar presents obstacles to passing the budget bill on schedule. As the session winds down in May and June—when the Legislature should be focused on its most important single responsibility, finalizing and completing the budget for delivery to the Governor—legislative policy and fiscal committees must contend with hundreds of substantive bills. Keeping track of legislative activities is difficult enough for legislative staff, full-time professional lobbyists and Sacramento media representatives. At a greater distance, it is almost impossible for members of the general public to stay informed about budget decisions, pending or already made.

Gubernatorial action—the Governor's final imprint

When the Governor receives the Legislature's version of the budget bill, the Constitution allows the chief executive only 12 days to decide whether to sign the bill as is, use a line-item veto to reduce or eliminate certain appropriations and associated budget control language,[41] or veto the entire bill (an extremely rare occurrence). Like emergency statutes passed by a two-thirds vote, the Budget Act becomes effective as soon as it is signed by the Governor.

The Legislature may override any line-item veto actions by a two-thirds vote of both houses, although such overrides rarely occur.

All state programs are impacted by the state budget.

The budget bill is the only piece of legislation that can contain more than one subject. Although it includes only "items of appropriation," the budget affects all aspects of state government—and, to a great extent, local government as well. The effectiveness of almost all state and state-funded local government programs

---

[40] The budget adoption deadline is earlier in the year in the majority of other states. (See Appendix C.)

[41] Almost all states provide for line-item vetoes by the Governor. (See Appendix D.)

depends largely upon their level of funding in the state budget. Involving the expenditure of almost $70 billion (in 1997-98), the final Budget Act typically runs to approximately 700 pages.

In addition to actual expenditure items, the Budget Act passed by the Legislature may include "control language" that affects how an appropriation can be used. In this way, the Legislature has the ability to influence implementation of a program without the necessity of actually amending the underlying statute that governs it. In some situations, however, statutory changes are needed to implement spending decisions in the Budget Act. During the early 1990s, for example, the Governor proposed reducing the grant amount to welfare recipients as well as freezing cost-of-living adjustments. These actions could not be taken solely in the Budget Act, since statutes controlled the amount appropriated in the budget. More than one dozen separate bills, known as budget implementation bills (or "trailer bills"), were needed to implement these spending reductions in the budget bill. Such bills often include significant policy changes which may not have been studied or debated in the regular policy committee process.

Fiscal interplay between the levels of government

Strings are often attached to the more than $30 billion of federal money that flows annually to state and local programs through the state budget. That tripartite relationship is currently in flux. The Welfare Reform Act of 1996 substantially reduced the level of federal control in the state welfare system, and other similar federal devolution proposals have been put forward in Congress.

Tensions also exist between the State and the various local government units—primarily counties and school districts—that actually spend approximately 75% of General Fund revenues. Just as federal subventions often come with limitations on how money may be spent, the State frequently imposes substantial restrictions and conditions on subventions to local government in state statutes (such as the Education Code and the Welfare and Institutions Code) and regulations, as well as in "control language" in the Budget Act itself or in the provisions of budget implementation bills.

In addition, the State's power to allocate property taxes—the principal local source of revenue for local government units—is highly controversial. Proposition 13 gave the State authority to allocate property tax revenues among local government entities. In 1993 and 1994, to ease its own budgetary pressures, the Legislature used that authority to shift property tax revenues from cities and counties to local school districts—thereby allowing the State to reduce the amount of state subventions to those districts required by Proposition 98. To limit such shifts in the future, several cities are considering a ballot initiative restricting the State's authority to shift property tax revenue away from cities to other local government entities.

Given the dynamic nature of politics and economics, it is unlikely that the complex fiscal relationships between the three levels of government will remain stable for any considerable length of time. Those responsible for enacting the state budget must be prepared for constant conflicts and pressures for adjustment and change in those relationships in the foreseeable future.

Conclusion

In seven of the past 10 years, the Governor and the Legislature have been unable to complete the budget by the July 1 start of the fiscal year, as required by the California Constitution. In 1992, as recession hit, the budget was not adopted and signed until 63 days into the new fiscal year. Considerable hardship resulted, as well as litigation over the issuance of special state warrants by the Controller to pay the State's bills during the delay.

As California emerged from the recession, it appeared that budgeting might become easier. However, the 1997-98 budget process demonstrates that scarcity of resources is not the only cause of budget delays. The 1997-98 budget, which contained sufficient resources to increase funding for existing state programs and start several new ones, was not signed until August 18, 1997—49 days late.

Negative reaction to those failures has been almost universal. An August 1997 Field Poll noted that the public is impatient with both the Governor and the Legislature.[42] The poll found that 31% of the respondents believed that the Governor had done a poor to very poor job in producing a budget, and 23% believed the same of the majority Democrats in the Legislature.

An often-proposed solution to budget delays is to penalize the Governor and the Legislature by withholding their salaries and expenses until the budget is adopted and signed.[43] Some have even suggested that the Controller should be forbidden by statute to make any payments until the budget is adopted. This solution is based on the presumption that it would bring state government operations to a halt and force prompt budget adoption. However, since most state spending is controlled by federal law and state constitutional provisions, any attempt to shut it down would probably be rendered largely moot by court orders based on those paramount federal and constitutional provisions.

The California Citizens Budget Commission believes that the deficiencies in the state budget process are more fundamental and can only be solved by a comprehensive program of reforms.

California's budget process can never return to the simplicity and comprehensibility that prevailed when its basic structures were created. The State's size and diversity create inherent problems of budgetary complexity. The same is

[42] The Field Institute, Release No. 1847 (August 26, 1997), page 3.
[43] See, for example, California Constitution Revision Commission, *Final Report and Recommendations to the Governor and the Legislature* (1996), page 44; ACA 1 (Goldsmith), ACA 21 (Papan), ACA 26 (Torlaksen) and SCA 16 (Lockyer), 1997-98 Session of the California Legislature.

true of the intricately intertwined fiscal relationships among federal, state and local governments. The nation's largest state will always have far more difficult budget problems than most other governmental units.

By the same token, the impact of Golden State politics on California's budgetary problems is beyond the purview of this Commission. There is no doubt that solutions to these problems are more difficult when there is, as has been the case almost constantly during the last 15 years, a partisan split between the Governor and the majorities in the Legislature. The close balance between Democrats and Republicans in the Legislature has also caused difficulty. This has been especially noticeable in the years when the Assembly was divided almost evenly between the parties, leading to contests for the Speakership which absorbed excessive amounts of attention and energy. In addition, term limits have reduced the institutional memory and the overall level of budgetary experience in both houses of the Legislature. Such political problems are inherent in any democratic system and will not be affected by the Commission's proposed reforms.

The Commission believes, however, that a number of very significant deficiencies in the budget process can be eliminated, or at least significantly moderated, by the comprehensive program of reforms recommended in Part III of this report.

California budget-makers can no longer assume, as many have in the past, that fiscal and budgetary problems will disappear with economic growth. Increases in the expenses of the most costly state programs will not necessarily be eliminated by revenue increases. The recent extensive expansion in proposed bond issues will ease fiscal pressures in the short run, but the large debt service expenses incurred must be paid for out of future revenues. In addition, bond financing generally covers only the capital costs of new facilities, not the additional operating costs those facilities entail.

The fundamental elements of the state budget process need to be reshaped to fit California's complex intergovernmental and fiscal relationships in the balance of this decade and on into the 21st century.

Part III

The Commission's Recommendations

The Commission's Recommendations

Introduction

The Commission's Preliminary Report was developed and issued during a period of great financial stress. As the Governor and the Legislature grappled with the problems resulting from California's most severe economic downturn since the 1930s, drastic measures were required to keep state and local government programs funded and the State endured four consecutive years of deficit spending. Accordingly, a good deal of the Preliminary Report focused on these budgetary difficulties. With California's economy on the upswing and the budget showing a surplus rather than a deficit, it is now possible to view the state budget process from a broader perspective.

California can be proud of many aspects of its state budget process. The Department of Finance and the Legislative Analyst's Office provide highly competent and professional services in the best tradition of government service. For the most part, the State follows Generally Accepted Accounting Principles (GAAP) in its budget presentation, and the high quality of its fiscal documentation is a model for state government financial reporting.[44] Fiscal forecasting is done in an objective and non-partisan manner that enables the State to avoid the partisan wrangling over budget estimates that so often poisons budget debates at all levels of government.

Nevertheless, serious defects in the state budget process require correction. Much of the process has been handed down from the days when California was a thinly populated agricultural state rather than the teeming economic colossus it is today. The Commission believes that stricter fiscal discipline is needed, especially during such times of economic downturn as the early 1990s. The Commission also believes that the budget should be adopted by the same simple majority vote

---

[44] See, for example, the Official Statements issued in connection with any of the recent state bond issues (available from the office of the State Treasurer). Pursuant to Chapter 1286, Statutes of 1984, the California State Accounting and Reporting System (CALSTARS) normally follows Generally Accepted Accounting Principles (GAAP). See Government Code Section 13306. Only 16 other states apply GAAP to budget documents. (See Appendix E.)

required for most major legislative decisions. In addition, the process should be more comprehensive, and focus more on the long-term consequences of budget decisions.

Budget information needs to be made more available to the public so that citizens may better understand the Sacramento budget decisions that so vitally affect their lives. Equally important, better accountability needs to be built into the budget system. Citizens should have both greater ability to determine the purposes of state programs and improved information about the effectiveness of those programs in achieving their stated purposes.

The Commission recognizes the limitations on what can be achieved through reform of the state budget process. Most basically, the Commission's recommendations concern process, not policy. They do not seek to establish the budgetary priorities that should be followed or the proper level of taxation for California. Those are political decisions properly left to the political process. Nor does this report follow the Commission's Preliminary Report in recommending a series of changes in state-local government fiscal relationships. That complex and controversial subject deserves to be dealt with more comprehensively than is possible in this report. Finally, the current effort of the federal government to "devolve" more authority for—as well as the accompanying fiscal control and responsibility over—state social welfare programs substantially financed with federal money is too new and too incomplete to be dealt with adequately as part of this report.

Recognizing these limitations, the Commission nevertheless feels strongly that unless significant improvements are made in the state budget process, California will continue on its present course of more and more "ballot-box budgeting." If indeed that continues, ultimately all major budget decisions will be dictated by constitutional provisions and statutory initiatives; the Governor and the Legislature will have little or no ability to deal with changing conditions, economic hard times or major emergencies. The citizens of California will suffer as a consequence, since it is their priorities the budget process should be geared to satisfy.

The recommendations set forth in this report, the Commission believes, can serve to give the voters and all Californians increased involvement and confidence in the budget process. With that increased public confidence, the pressure for more "budgeting by initiative" should be reduced; and our elected officials will be better positioned to meet the fiscal challenges that will confront California in the 21ˢᵗ century.

In Appendix J of this report, the Commission has set forth proposed language for the constitutional and statutory changes that would be required to implement these recommendations.

California should balance its state budget more rigorously.

During the recession of the early 1990s, California's fiscal problems were the focus of intense debate. Today, with the State's current economy healthy once again, scrutiny of California's budget structure and fiscal condition has greatly diminished. While increasing revenues have enabled California to eliminate the deficit accumulated during the recession, the State's flawed budget process remains basically the same. The process lacks the fiscal discipline needed if the budget is to meet the needs of a growing state through good times and bad. The current budget process has no constitutional requirement that expenditures and revenues be balanced, fails to include large amounts of state spending, and allows short-term and "off-budget" borrowing to facilitate deficit spending.

The Commission recommends five changes to end such practices and impose stricter fiscal discipline on California's budgeting process.

1. All future state budgets should be balanced—as presented, passed and signed into law.

2. External short-term borrowing to finance a deficit should be prohibited, except as voted by a 60% majority in both houses of the Legislature in carefully defined circumstances.

3. Long-term debt should be used only to finance capital items.

4. Off-budget state expenditures and borrowing should be prohibited.

5. The Joint Legislative Budget Committee should monitor implementation of the budget and recommend changes to keep the budget in balance. In the absence of corrective action by the Legislature, the Governor should have the authority to make expenditure reductions to balance the budget.

Recommendation 1:
Broaden and Strengthen Balanced-Budget Requirements

The annual Budget Act constitutes the statutory spending plan for California. The California Constitution requires the Governor to *submit* a balanced budget to the Legislature each year, but it does not require the Legislature to *pass* a balanced budget or the Governor to *sign* a balanced budget. In short, the Constitution does not require the Budget Act to be balanced.

A balanced budget is a sound fiscal goal. Fairness dictates that taxpayers pay for the programs carried out for their benefit, not pass along the costs of those programs to future generations of taxpayers by borrowing to finance a gap between current revenues and current expenditures. When this happens, the substantial cost of any deficit financing is also passed along to future taxpayers.

The repeated failure of the Governor and the Legislature to make the hard choices needed to produce a balanced budget can have a disastrous cumulative effect. If it is permissible to spend in excess of revenues plus reserves, the Legislature acts on spending demands without benefit of the most compelling reason for withholding approval: the need to ration scarce revenue resources. If the bill for today's services can be passed along to future taxpayers, resources are no longer scarce.

> **Problem:**
> **California's Constitution**
> **does not require a**
> **balanced budget.**

The lack of fiscal discipline can become habitual, making budget balance ever harder to achieve. Repeated small deficits, combined with the cost of financing the resulting debt, become a large problem. Such practices, combined with a downturn in the economy, can result in acute financial distress for the State and for the education, health, social welfare, public safety and other programs which depend on its financial support.

As a practical matter, the State of California, like all states, has no realistic alternative to a balanced-budget policy. No state has the fiscal and monetary tools or the tax base that enable the federal government to run up large deficits over long periods. States cannot print money and do not have the borrowing capacity to incur the multi-trillion dollar debt levels incurred by the federal government during the 1980s. Nor do the states have the responsibility or the capability of using the fiscal and monetary tools employed at the federal level for major countercyclical spending to reduce the impact of economic downturns. Repeated deficit spending at the state level will result in higher interest costs on larger amounts of debt leading inevitably to tax increases and the flight of the business tax base on which so much state revenue depends.

California has long recognized the importance of balanced budgets. As pointed out above, the state budget initially presented by the Governor to the Legislature must be balanced.[45] State statutory law prohibits the annual Budget Act from making appropriations in excess of projected revenues and states the intent of the Legislature that spending not exceed revenues.[46] California statutory law also requires counties and school districts to have balanced budgets.

The Legislature and the Governor do endeavor to balance the budget each year, recognizing that out-of-balance budgets do not reflect favorably on lawmakers and Governors. This balanced-budget policy does, even during a recessionary period of low revenues and increasing program costs, put downward pressure on program growth and constrain spending. As California entered the recent recession, the projected budget shortfall in 1991-92 totaled $14 billion. That fiscal year's budget solution consisted largely of a combination of expenditure reductions and revenue increases. As the recession continued, the State faced annual budget shortfalls of varying magnitude, and pressure to reduce expenditures continued. As a result,

---

[45] California Constitution, Article IV, Subsection 12(a).
[46] Section 13337.5 of the Government Code.

General Fund expenditures for 1992-93 and 1993-94 actually declined from 1991-92 levels, despite continued population growth and increased program costs.

Nearly all states have some form of a balanced-budget requirement. In 45 states, the Governor must submit a balanced-budget proposal to the Legislature; in 40 states, the Legislature must pass a balanced budget; and in 32 states, the budget signed by the Governor must be balanced. (See Appendix F.)

The Commission recommends that California join the great majority of states with true balanced-budget requirements and require that all future state budgets have a balanced General Fund as presented to the Legislature, passed by the Legislature and enacted into law. Subject to the narrow exception provided for emergency situations in Recommendation No. 2, projected General Fund spending should not exceed projected revenues and available reserves for any budget cycle. The Commission believes a constitutional balanced-budget requirement would provide the State with a needed increase in fiscal discipline.

The Commission sees no easy solution to the problem of enforcing a constitutional state balanced-budget requirement. In a 1992 survey by the National Association of State Budget Officers, 22 states reported that they had enforcement provisions associated with their balanced-budget requirements; yet 13 of those states cited "tradition" as their enforcement mechanism rather than any specific statutory or constitutional provision.[47]

Most experts reject the idea of having the courts enforce balanced-budget requirements. Litigation is too cumbersome and time-consuming to be an effective enforcement tool, and would raise separation-of-powers issues if used as the means to force a balanced budget. In fact, no cases have been reported in any state in the last several decades in which taxpayers have succeeded in securing judicial enforcement of balanced-budget constitutional provisions.[48]

The Commission concludes that the best approach to enforcing the balanced-budget requirement would be to spell out the balanced-budget principles and requirements in the California Constitution and allow the people to enforce them through the regular political processes. Governors and legislators will be wary of violating constitutional provisions that have been passed by a vote of the people and will, presumably, pay a political price for doing so.

> ## The Commission's Recommendation:
> All future state budgets—as presented by the Governor, passed by the Legislature and signed by the Governor—should be required to have a balanced General Fund. Budgeted General Fund expenditures should not exceed estimated revenues for the budget cycle. (Constitutional change)

---

[47] National Association of State Budget Officers, *State Balanced Budget Requirements: Provisions and Practices* (June 24, 1992), page 5.
[48] Briffault, *Balancing Acts—The Reality Behind State Balanced Budget Requirements,* 20th Century Fund (1996), pages 39-40.

Recommendation 2:
Prohibit External Borrowing

Article XVI, Section 1 of the California Constitution stipulates that the Legislature must not create a debt exceeding the sum of $300,000 without a vote of the people.

Problem: California's state government avoids balancing its budget by borrowing to finance operating expenses.

However, in 1933, the California Supreme Court ruled that the State could borrow money for cash flow purposes as long as there was reasonable certainty that funds would be available to repay the borrowed money within a short period. During the Great Depression of the 1930s, the State borrowed up to 20% of the General Fund to cover budget deficits that continued for ten years.

During the recession of the early 1990s, the State followed the judicial rules laid down in the 1930s and financed four years of budget deficits by borrowing from private capital markets. (See Table 13.) Conditions were finally placed on the State's borrowing practices in 1994-95, when California borrowed a record $4 billion from institutional lenders to meet its fiscal obligations. Concerned about the State's fiscal and budgetary situation, the financial markets imposed various conditions and requirements as prerequisites for loans, including automatic budget reduction mechanisms and other guarantees.

Table 13:
Borrowing to Finance a Deficit

1991-92 to 1995-96
(Millions)

Fiscal Year	Amount Borrowed	Percent of the General Fund
1991-92	475	1.1%
1992-93	2,000	4.6%
1993-94	3,200	8.2%
1994-95*	4,000	n/a

*Financed a two-year budget

**Source: State Fiscal Condition Report
Little Hoover Commission, March 1995**

The Commission believes that the State should not have to rely on outside lending institutions to impose needed fiscal discipline. The State's borrowing practices should be governed by its own constitutional and statutory provisions, in accordance with sound financial principles. The Commission, therefore, recommends that the Constitution be amended to prohibit all external short-term borrowing, unless it is used to meet the State's normal cashflow fluctuations and is repaid within the same or next budget year from designated revenues.[49] This would allow external short-term borrowing to meet cash-flow needs, while eliminating such borrowing for deficit financing purposes. As of 1992, only a dozen other states allowed year-end deficits to be carried over into following years and financed by

---

[49] The ability to repay short-term external borrowing within a two-year period would coordinate with the two-year budget cycle recommended by the Commission in Recommendation 14.

debt arrangements.[50] The Commission believes California should join the majority of states that do not permit such practices.

The State Treasurer regularly borrows from state special funds for the General Fund, and among various special funds and similar accounts, for cash flow purposes. Such borrowing is limited to moneys that may be temporarily available in those funds and is controlled by the constitutional and statutory provisions governing expenditures from them. The use of such temporarily available moneys is appropriate and cost effective when the borrowing costs are lower than the costs of equivalent external borrowing. Such internal state borrowing should be regularly reported, as provided in Recommendations 11 and 12, but does not present the same danger as external borrowing. This distinction is also made in the equivalent recommendation of the California Constitution Revision Commission.[51]

The Commission recognizes that emergency situations, such as the severe recession suffered by the State in the early 1990s, may occasionally make necessary some longer-term deficit financing. This Recommendation does, therefore, allow a 60% majority of both houses of the Legislature to carry over short-term debt to later budget periods to meet such defined emergency situations, provided the Governor concurs. A two-thirds majority vote would still be required to override a gubernatorial veto of a budget including such extraordinary borrowing. The Commission believes that such provisions should provide adequate safeguards for dealing with severe economic conditions or other major budgetary emergencies.

The Commission's Recommendation:

External borrowing to finance a General Fund deficit should be prohibited, except to meet legitimate cash flow needs within the current and immediately succeeding budget year. Rollover of such short-term debt to any later budget year should occur only in the event of defined emergency circumstances voted by a 60% majority of both houses of the Legislature. (Constitutional change)

Recommendation 3:
Limit Long-Term Debt

> *Problem:*
> *There is no limitation on the uses of long-term financing.*

The Commission believes that long-term borrowing (more than five years) is appropriate to finance public investments that provide long-term public benefits, such as highways, parks or state buildings, as long as projected revenues can service the debt. In addition, using debt to finance income-

---

[50] National Association of State Budget Officers, *State Balanced Budget Requirements: Provisions and Practices* (June 24, 1992), page 1.
[51] California Constitution Revision Commission, *Final Report and Recommendations to the Governor and the Legislature (1996)*, pages 42-43.

generating facilities, such as toll bridges, allows the State to construct such facilities now and pay for them with revenues they generate in the future.

The State Constitution, however, contains no limit on the uses to which bond proceeds can be put. The proceeds of voter-approved state general obligation bond issues (but not from lease-revenue bond issues which do not require voter approval) can be used for any purpose, including payment of operating expenses or deficit financing. The Commission believes that multi-year borrowing for operating expenses or similar uses is a poor management practice. Such borrowing simply shifts current expenses to become the obligation of future taxpayers who do not enjoy the benefits of the expenditures. Therefore, the Commission recommends that the Constitution be amended to limit long-term debt to the financing of long-term capital investments.

The Commission's Recommendation:
Long-term debt should be limited to capital items. (Constitutional change)

Recommendation 4:
Prohibit Off-Budget Transactions

"Off-budget" transactions are a common method of avoiding state balanced-budget requirements. Studies have shown that in most states with such requirements, only one-half to three-quarters of state spending is subject to those requirements.[52] California is one of those states with extensive "off-budget" borrowing and spending.

> **Problem:**
> **Off-budget transactions conceal the State's true financial condition from the public.**

During the budget crises of the early 1990s, the State provided "off-budget loans" to K-12 schools to maintain per-pupil spending at the 1991-92 level. Those "loans" were to be "repaid" by schools from future appropriations required by the appropriation guarantees of Proposition 98.[53] The primary purpose of the "loans" was to maintain schools at the prior year funding level without exceeding the existing minimum funding level, which would have invoked Proposition 98's requirement to increase future school funding.[54]

The loans were termed "off-budget" because they never appeared in the accounting of state debt. Financed through short-term borrowing, the loans were a form   of

---

[52] Briffault, Balancing Acts: *The Reality Behind State Balanced Budget Requirements*, 20ᵗʰ Century Fund (1996), pages 11-14.
[53] Legislative Analyst's Office, *Proposed Settlement Agreement of CTA v. Gould* (1996).
[54] Passed in November 1988, Proposition 98 amended the State Constitution and added sections to the Education Code. For a full description of its requirements, see the Legislative Analyst's Office publication, *The 1991-92 Budget, Perspectives and Issues*, pages 143-57.

deficit spending. The schools successfully challenged the repayment requirement in the courts. The trial court found that the bulk of "off-budget loans" to schools were, in effect, appropriations that raised the Proposition 98 funding requirements for subsequent budget years.

The Commission recommends that all such "off-budget" borrowing and expenditures be prohibited.[55] They are inappropriate because they obscure the State's true fiscal condition and make it difficult for the public to hold decisionmakers accountable for their actions. In addition, the Commission strongly suggests that the reasons for any legitimate loan, along with provisions for its repayment, be explicitly stated in the law authorizing the loan.

The Commission's Recommendation:

Off-budget state expenditures and borrowing should be constitutionally prohibited. (Constitutional change)

Recommendation 5:
Increase Authority to Maintain a Balanced Budget

A balanced-budget requirement cannot ensure that the budget will *remain* balanced, especially if the State follows Recommendation 14 and shifts to a two-year budget cycle. Significant fiscal changes may occur after the budget is enacted which would put it out of balance before the end of the cycle. Expenditures are hard to project accurately, especially for new programs, and the State's two main revenue sources—personal income taxes and sales taxes—are relatively volatile.

Even during the recent recession, when revenues plummeted and expenditures rose, the Legislature and the Governor produced budgets that were balanced—at least on paper. The budgets for those fiscal years, however, did not *remain* balanced. For many years, California has ended each year with a deficit.[56]

It is important that the Governor, the Legislature and the public be kept fully informed of the status of state expenditures and revenues, so that timely action can be taken in the event that an imbalance develops. In addition to monitoring the status of the state budget for the Governor and the Legislature as they currently do, the Commission recommends that the Department of Finance (DOF) and the Joint Legislative Budget Committee (JLBC) should be given the statutory responsibility of issuing periodic reports to inform the public of the budget's current status.

---

[55] As a result of the *CTA v. Gould* case (Sacramento Superior Court Case No. 373-415) (Third District Court of Appeal, 3 Civil, No. 018-447), the State has already agreed not to make "off-budget loans" to the schools of the type referred to in the two preceding paragraphs. Such a requirement is part of the settlement agreement and final judgment in the *Gould* case (dated July 25, 1996). That agreement was formally approved by the Legislature (Chapter 78, Statutes of 1996).

[56] Chart D in the Background Information provided with the Governor's proposed 1998-99 budget, available on the Department of Finance website at http://www.dof.ca.gov (from the DOF home page, click on California Budget, then FAQs, then Background Information).

> **Problem:**
> **Effective mechanisms are needed to keep the General Fund budget in balance during the budget cycle.**

The information reported by the DOF at the time the Governor's new budget is presented in January, and the Legislative Analyst's subsequent analysis of that budget (as the agent of the JLBC) are now the most comprehensive such reports. The Commission believes that the DOF should also make a particular effort to see that the information presented with the Governor's so-called May Revision of the proposed budget includes comprehensive information about the status of the current budget. That information should be widely distributed to the media and the public in a format easily understood by those concerned with the state budget process.

The Commission further recommends that the JLBC be given the statutory responsibility for recommending any changes needed to keep the budget in balance after it is enacted—particularly during the interim period after the Legislature recesses for the year. Those recommendations should be made available to the media and the public. They could spark an ongoing public debate about the State's fiscal condition to help the Legislature make the revenue and expenditure decisions needed to maintain a balanced budget.

Many states assign that responsibility to the Governor—mandating or allowing the Governor to impose spending reductions within a specified range during the fiscal year. (See Appendix G.) Some of the states with such provisions require Governors to make any reductions on an "across-the-board" percentage basis. The Commission considered, but rejected, this alternative. Arbitrary "across-the-board" spending reductions tend to create a myriad of other problems. In fact, some programs can accommodate cuts better than others.

The Commission believes it is wiser to encourage thoughtful deliberation between the Governor and the Legislature than to enact arbitrary "trigger" mechanisms. Unlike the many states with part-time Legislatures, California's Legislature meets for eight months or more each year and is capable of initiating mid-course corrections to keep the budget in balance. In the absence of action by the Legislature to balance the budget, however, the Commission recommends that the Governor be given the statutory authority, after 30 days written notice to the Legislature, to make expenditure reductions as necessary to maintain a balanced budget.

It should be noted that the Governor's authority under this recommendation would be quite limited. As set forth in Part II, the majority of state spending is done pursuant to state constitutional requirements or through programs partially funded by the federal government. The statutory authority being exercised by the Governor would, obviously, be subordinate both to relevant state constitutional provisions and to any federal statute governing federally supported programs.

The Commission's Recommendation:

During both legislative sessions and interim periods, the Joint Legislative Budget Committee should have the responsibility of recommending any legislative actions needed to keep the budget in balance. In the absence of corrective action by the Legislature, the Governor should have the authority to make such expenditure reductions as are needed to maintain the balance.
(Statutory change)

The state budget process should be governed by majority vote.

California is one of only two states which require a two-thirds vote of each house of the Legislature to pass the Budget Act. (See Appendix H.) Budget implementation bills, which take effect simultaneously with the Budget Act, also require a two-thirds vote. In addition, while tax expenditures (exemptions, credits and other tax preferences) can be enacted by a majority vote in the Legislature, they require a two-thirds vote for repeal.

The two-thirds vote requirement for budget adoption has been in effect since 1933 when the voters approved a constitutional amendment establishing a spending limit for the State. If the budget exceeded the limit, a two-thirds vote was required. In the 1960s, the Constitution Revision Commission recommended that the spending limit be removed, but the two-thirds vote requirement retained. This recommendation was submitted to the voters and approved; the two-thirds requirement remains in the State Constitution today.

The Commission concludes that this super-majority vote requirement has not fulfilled its original purpose; rather, it has worked to the detriment of the State's budget process. The Commission, therefore, recommends that the Budget Act be adopted by a simple majority vote. The Commission further recommends that the majority vote requirement be applied to the adoption of budget implementation bills and to the repeal of tax expenditures.

Related recommendations to make the budget and fiscal process more open and democratic include focusing legislative and public attention on the budget at the time of its adoption and establishing a process for the review and reconsideration of the many constraints that currently limit the scope of the state budget process.

Five recommendations address majority votes and related issues.

6. The Constitution should be amended to require only a simple majority vote for the adoption of the budget

7. Legislation needed to implement the budget should be treated as part of the budget.

8. The vote requirements to create or repeal tax expenditures should be the same: a simple majority vote.

9. The adoption of the budget should be the only item on the legislative agenda for the period immediately prior to its adoption.

10. Meaningful reviews of all constitutional and statutory expenditure and revenue constraints should be conducted and reports issued on a regular basis by the Joint Legislative Budget Committee and an independent citizens commission.

Recommendation 6:
Enact Budget by Simple Majority

Some experts have sought to justify California's two-thirds vote requirement for the adoption of the state budget as a way to prevent excessive state spending. The Commission believes, however, that a super-majority requirement may have the opposite effect and result in increased state spending. A small group of legislators can as easily withhold the votes necessary for a two-thirds majority to obtain an increase in spending on their favorite programs as to obtain a decrease in spending.[57] There is no evidence that the two-thirds vote requirement does anything to slow the growth in state

> **Problem:**
> **The two-thirds vote requirement for the adoption of the budget impedes the budget process.**

spending. Instead, it allows a minority to frustrate the process of reaching compromises that are essential to putting a budget together.

The super-majority vote requirement for the budget also obscures who is responsible for budget decisions. As long as a super-majority vote is required to pass and send the budget to the Governor, the public has difficulty determining which legislators or political parties are responsible for either creating or resolving a fiscal imbalance.

After considerable research and discussion, the Commission recommends that the Constitution be amended to provide for adoption of the state budget by a simple majority vote of the Legislature.[58]

A super-majority vote requirement may be appropriate in special situations, such as when the Legislature seeks to override the Governor's veto. The regular budget bill, however, provides general support for the ordinary operations of state government and is hedged with numerous safeguards to prevent abuse. The Governor must present the Legislature with a balanced spending plan; the budget

---

[57] As pointed out in the Commission's Preliminary Report (Table 15 and accompanying text, pages 43-44), during the last 30 years budget impasses between the Governor and the Legislature have as often resulted in budget increases as decreases.

[58] The great majority of other states require only simple majorities in the Legislature to pass the budget bill. (See Appendix H.)

must be adopted by a date specified in the Constitution; and the Governor is vested with line-item veto power over each appropriation. Finally, unlike other legislation, the budget bill is in effect for only one year and generally does not create new programs. All of those attributes support the view that a super-majority vote requirement is unnecessary to prevent excessive state spending.[59]

The Commission's Recommendation:

The state budget should be enacted by a simple majority vote of the two houses of the Legislature. (Constitutional change)

Recommendation 7: Treat Implementation Bills as Part of the Budget

Budget implementation bills ("trailer bills") are part of the state budget process and reflect the same policies as those underlying the budget bill itself. Budget implementation bills go into effect with the enactment of the budget and, like the Budget Act, require a two-thirds vote. However, in acting on these bills, the Governor has no line-item veto comparable to the power that he or she has with respect to the budget bill. The Governor can only sign or veto the entire implementation bill, not withhold approval of specific provisions of the legislation.

> *Problem:*
> *The two-thirds vote requirement for implementation bills causes the same problems as with the budget bill itself.*

Since the sole function of budget implementation bills is to put the Budget Act into effect, those bills should be subject to the same rules as the budget bill. The Commission recommends, therefore, that budget implementation bills also be adopted by a simple majority vote of the Legislature. Passage of such trailer bills by majority vote would make it easier to enact a budget. The contents of those bills should be limited to items that are related to and necessary for the implementation of appropriations contained in the budget (and not used as a substitute for substantive legislation unrelated to the fiscal policy matters involved in the budget).

In addition, the Commission recommends that the Governor be allowed to veto specific items in trailer bills in the exact same way as the Governor can now veto line-item budget bill appropriations and associated language. Just as budget implementation bills should not go beyond matters directly related to such implementation, so the Governor's line-item veto power should be limited to matters connected with appropriations vetoed, and not used broadly to affect

---

[59] The 1996 Report of the California Constitution Revision Commission makes the same majority vote for budget adoption recommendation. Op. cit., footnote 51, pages 43-44.

unrelated policy matters. The Legislature's power to override such vetoes by a two-thirds vote should also be retained.

The budget is the one document that reflects the Governor's policy agenda. Allowing specific statutory language, as well as related budget appropriations, to be vetoed would enhance the Governor's power to shape overall budget policy. It would also allow the public to determine more easily who is accountable for the final form of the budget.

Finally, the Commission believes that budget implementation bills should not be subject to the single-subject rule, as they currently are. Trailer bills often involve complex subject matter and should not be so limited as long as they are genuinely germane to actual budget implementation.

> ## The Commission's Recommendation:
> **Budget implementation bills should be treated as part of the state budget: adopted by majority vote, subject to the line-item veto and not limited by the single-subject rule.** (Constitutional change)

Recommendation 8:
Enact and Repeal Tax Expenditures By Simple Majority

The Legislature can adopt tax expenditures by a simple majority vote. To eliminate or reduce those tax benefits, however, requires a two-thirds super-majority vote— the same vote needed to enact a new tax or increase an existing tax. Thus it is relatively easy to enact tax expenditures, but very difficult to repeal them.

As set forth in Recommendation 11, the Commission recommends that existing tax expenditures—primarily tax exemptions, credits and deductions—be incorporated into the budget process and evaluated together with state spending programs. The effect of such tax preferences is, in economic terms, the same as direct government spending. These preferences can now be created by majority votes in the Legislature, the same vote requirement the Commission recommends for adoption of the budget. The Commission recommends that the alteration, reduction or repeal of tax breaks should require the same majority vote.

> *Problem:*
> *Vote requirements for increasing and decreasing tax expenditures are inconsistent.*

The current requirement for a two-thirds vote in both houses of the Legislature makes any effort at tax simplification, or the removal of any of the hundreds of tax preferences cluttering the Revenue and Taxation Code, next to impossible.

This recommendation should not be interpreted as meaning that the Commission supports a change in the two-thirds requirement for enacting new taxes or increasing existing tax levels. To the contrary, a number of Commission members feel strongly that the two-thirds requirement for the enactment of new State taxes, contained in Section 3 of Proposition 13 (California Constitution, Article XIII-A), should remain in place. The continuing wide public support for Proposition 13 makes it unlikely, in any event, that the two-thirds requirement of Section 3 will be reduced or repealed at any time in the foreseeable future.

> ## The Commission's Recommendation:
> **Tax expenditures should be created, modified or repealed in accordance with the same vote requirement: a majority vote of the Legislature.**
> (Constitutional change)

Recommendation 9:
Focus Legislative Activity on the Budget in June

High-profile issues, such as affirmative action and "three strikes" sentencing, get the lion's share of the media and public attention devoted to state government problems. Budget matters are generally noticed only when they involve emotional issues, such as Medi-Cal funding for abortions, or when the budget is late.

> **Problem:**
> *Basic budget decision-making does not receive the public and legislative attention it deserves.*

The public normally is not involved in details of spending and revenue debates during the annual budget process. Obscure terminology, inadequate information and an opaque process effectively exclude the average person, leaving the public with little understanding of, or ability to influence, spending and revenue choices made in Sacramento.

Requiring the Legislature to devote all its attention to the budget in the period prior to the June 15 adoption deadline would better focus public attention on budget issues. If the ban on other business was required to continue until adoption of the budget, this requirement might also assist in getting the budget adopted in a timely manner.[60] The Commission, therefore, suggests to the Legislature that it give serious consideration to the adoption of this recommendation as a way to increase public understanding of, and participation in, the state budget process.

> ## The Commission's Recommendation:
> **In even-numbered years, the legislative session should have a period, beginning June 1 and ending with the passage of the Budget Act, when adoption of the budget would be the only order of business.** (Constitutional change)

[60] It was suggested during the Commission process that this recommendation go one step further, and provide that the session would come to an automatic end if the Budget were not adopted in a timely manner; all pending items not already enacted would die, and the Legislature would start at ground zero in its next regular or special session.

Recommendation 10:
Institute Regular Independent Review of Budget Constraints

California's budget system is replete with restrictions on the authority of the Governor and the Legislature to control spending through the annual budget process. The principal restrictions consist of special funds and various funding guarantees.

Special funds are established to receive dedicated tax revenues and expend them for specific purposes. (See Table 7.) Both the Legislature and the voters have increasingly used special funds to direct state spending. The Legislature has often tied its own hands by transferring general-purpose tax revenue into special accounts.

Acting through the ballot initiative process, the public has also imposed broad constraints on various revenues (such as with Proposition 13, which limited tax increases) and created mandatory spending programs (such as with Proposition 98, which provided a minimum funding guarantee for K-12 education and community colleges). The cumulative effects of these actions has severely limited state budget choices and made it increasingly difficult for decision-makers to meet the needs and desires of the public. While these initiatives reflected priorities of the public when they were adopted, circumstances invariably change, and the public's priorities change with them. Today it is exceedingly difficult for the public to review or modify earlier initiatives unless the Legislature first places amendments to them on the ballot or unless new initiatives are qualified to amend or repeal past measures.

Some argue that special funding serves a critical role in the State's financing and agenda-setting. With the Legislature often locked in indecision over alternative ways to appropriate and spend the State's limited General Fund revenues, dedicated funding offers a method by which important state services—education, law enforcement, health, transportation—can receive dedicated and sustained funding.

> **Problem:**
> *California law greatly constrains the authority of the Governor and the Legislature to determine public spending policy.*

The increased use of special funds, however, is not without problems. In times of fiscal crisis, important General Fund programs—such as higher education—must be cut, while what may be considered less important dedicated funds remain intact or even in surplus. Special fund and priority measures in the aggregate have drastically curtailed state government's discretion to make budgeting and other fiscal decisions. Elected state officials and the public, however, have no regular process for assessing the cumulative impact of the numerous limitations on the state budget process (summarized in Part II).

For these reasons, the Commission recommends that in each legislative session, the Joint Legislative Budget Committee review the cumulative fiscal impact of constitutional and statutory spending and revenue constraints affecting the state budget and recommend appropriate changes. If California switches to a two-year budget cycle, as the Commission recommends, such a review could best be done in the off-years in which the entire state budget is not being considered and adopted by the Legislature.

In addition, the Commission believes that the state government and the voters should have some regular procedure for an outside, independent body to review all restrictions on the budget process, consider whether priorities have changed over time, and assess the need for possible modifications. For that reason, the Commission recommends that an independent group, similar to the Constitution Revision Commission, be formed at least once during each gubernatorial term to review California fiscal policy as a whole and present to state officials and the public recommendations for modifications to meet current state needs. To give added weight to those recommendations where they involve the State Constitution, the Commission recommends that any proposed constitutional amendment resulting from the proposed review process should be subject to adoption by majority vote of the Legislature (rather than by the two-thirds vote normally required for constitutional amendments).

The Commission's Recommendation:

In every budget cycle, the Joint Legislative Budget Committee should review and issue a report on the fiscal impact of all constitutional and statutory expenditure and revenue constraints on the state budget process. On a quadrennial basis, an independent body should be created to conduct a similar review (to include all continuing appropriations and special funds) and recommend appropriate modifications of those constraints to the Legislature. The Legislature should be authorized, acting by majority vote, to submit to a vote of the people such of those recommendations as involve constitutional amendments. (Constitutional and statutory changes)

The state budget process should be comprehensive, accessible and long-term oriented.

The state budget process should not be left to the select few who fully understand the intricacies of building and adopting the budget. The voters, the taxpayers, the press and everyone interested in public affairs should have ready access to the information they need to understand and evaluate budget decisions being made by the Governor and the Legislature.

The documentation and analysis of the annual state budget currently provided to the Governor by the Department of Finance (DOF), and to the Legislature by the Legislative Analyst's Office, are commendably thorough and detailed. The Commission believes these practices should be continued by the State on a permanent basis and recommends that a comprehensive state budget process be constitutionally mandated.

In order to ensure the availability to the public of the most important elements of this budget information, the Commission recommends that the Budget Act itself include a statement of the State's total fiscal condition and a complete summary of all state spending and revenues. Similarly, tax expenditures are now reported annually by the DOF but not formally included in the state budget process. The Commission believes that they should be included in the process, and should also be listed in the Budget Act.

Another major flaw in the present budget process is its short planning horizon. Currently, the budget is an annual event that begins again as soon as the last budget is concluded. Major state responsibilities, such as higher education and criminal justice, would benefit from a longer budget period, which would provide a greater level of certainty and program stability.

To correct these deficiencies, the Commission developed the following recommendations.

11. The state budget process should be comprehensive and include complete fiscal information for all state-funded programs. The Budget Act itself should contain a summary of that information as well as a simple Statement of Fiscal Condition for the State.

12. Tax expenditures should be a regular part of the state budget process and should be listed in the Budget Act.

13. The State should provide an easily understood budget summary widely available to the public and a budget primer to be distributed annually to taxpayers.

14. The State should adopt a two-year budget cycle.

15. A long-term spending plan, including a capital investment budget, should be included in the state budget.

Recommendation 11:
Make the Budget Process All-Inclusive

The fiscal information presented annually by the Governor with the state budget in January is both extensive and detailed. The analysis of the Governor's budget documents done by the Legislative Analyst's Office is also impressively professional and thorough. The Commission commends the Department of Finance and the Analyst's Office for the high quality of their budget presentations and analyses and believes that this high level of budget information should be constitutionally mandated so that it will be a permanent feature of California's state budget process.

> **Problem:**
> **Much important budgetary information is not formally included in the state budget process.**

The Commission recommends that this constitutional mandate specifically require that the state budget process include all projected expenditures, revenues and tax expenditures, as well as all projected subventions to and transfers from other levels of government.

> **The Commission's Recommendation:**
> California should have a unified and comprehensive state budget process. All projected expenditures, revenues and tax expenditures (including all subventions to and transfers from other levels of government) should be included in that process. (Constitutional change)

Recommendation 12:
Make Important Budget Information Readily Accessible

As presented to the Legislature in January, the Governor's Budget includes a very broad range of fiscal information. However, only a limited number of budget specialists in the Legislature and the Department of Finance (DOF) are familiar enough with the many complex schedules and other documents included in that Budget, and in its legislative review and change, to have a comprehensive overview of the State's overall budget and fiscal situation. Members of the public do not have adequate access to the critical information they need to understand the State's budget picture.

> **Problem:**
> *Important fiscal information is not included in the Budget Act, making it very difficult for the public to obtain the information needed to understand the decisions being made and to hold budget-makers accountable.*

The Commission believes that special sections of the Budget Act itself should set forth key elements of the State's budgetary and fiscal situation, giving the public an opportunity to better understand the state budget and the decisions that need to be made to finalize the budget. Therefore, the Commission recommends that the following three sections be required by statute to be included in the Budget Act. The included information should be current as of the date the Budget Act is adopted. Using that date would allow for the use of the best available information close to the start of the budget year, as well as for adjustments for legislation passed prior to the enactment of the budget.

(a) *Listing of All Tax Expenditures* California allocates resources for public purposes in two different ways: it spends tax revenues to finance public programs, and it promotes specific kinds of spending by private individuals and businesses by exempting them from the basic taxation structure through tax breaks. (See the Tax Expenditures section of Part II.) During state budget debates, however, such tax preferences are not central to the deliberations because they are not formally itemized as part of the budget. Once granted, they often continue in perpetuity and are relatively isolated from the public scrutiny and debate involved in the regular budget process.

In 1991, the Legislative Analyst found significant gaps in the supporting information and clarity of purpose with respect to many of the hundreds of tax expenditures catalogued. She concluded that the Legislature needed to review and agree upon the rationales, objectives and effectiveness of each tax expenditure. The Analyst further argued that the Legislature needed to set relative priorities for tax expenditures as a whole in order to consider the need to eliminate or modify some tax preferences.[61] While some bills have been introduced to require tax expenditures to be formally integrated into the budget process so that overall priorities can be set, no legislation along these lines has been enacted.

The Commission recommends that tax expenditures be listed in a separate section of the Budget Act[62] and formally included as part of budget

---

[61] Legislative Analyst's Office, *Analysis of the 1991-92 Tax Expenditure Budget: Overview and Compendium of Individual Tax Expenditure Programs* (1991), pages 9-12. A new study of tax expenditures is to be published in 1998.

[62] As presented by the Governor in January, this listing of tax expenditures could not include the latest information from the Franchise Tax Board's tax model, normally updated at the end of the calendar year. That information could be included with the May Revision to the Governor's Budget. Even when the budget is adopted, the effect of recently enacted revenue and expenditure changes might not be included. Such omissions should not materially detract from the overall usefulness of the listing.

deliberations.[63] The listing should include the estimated revenue loss and number of taxpayers affected by each tax expenditure. A balanced budget would be more easily achieved if the Governor and Legislature were able to consider all the relevant and available fiscal choices. Decision-makers should not contemplate either raising general tax rates or cutting public services without being able to assess the comparative value of eliminating or modifying specific tax preferences. Inclusion of tax expenditures would provide the information necessary to consider and establish overall priorities for all forms of spending.

(b) *Statement of Fiscal Condition* Although state budgeting and debt management involve two different governmental functions, the radical changes in California's fiscal condition during this decade illustrate the need for a single point in the fiscal decision-making process where the overall financial condition of the State is reported in a manner that can be understood by the public. This information is included in the detailed documentation that accompanies the Governor's Budget, and is available on the Internet through the DOF Website.[64] However, familiarity with the detail of the state budget process is needed to access that information, and no statutory mandate requires it to be provided in a manner easily available to the public.

To provide ready public access, the Commission recommends that a "Statement of Fiscal Condition" be contained in a separate section of each year's Budget Act, including estimated revenues and expenditures, short-term internal and external borrowing with associated debt-service costs for the most recently completed fiscal year, and current long-term borrowing with associated debt-service costs.

The Commission believes that this Statement should be an essential element in all annual budget decision making. This new section of the Budget Act would facilitate close monitoring of the fiscal health of the State, an important consideration in the budget process. The public, as well as the State's elected officials, would be able to assess the State's overall fiscal condition as decisions on individual spending programs are made. A weakened cash position, requiring excessive external borrowing, could provide an early warning of impending fiscal and budgetary problems.

The DOF and the State Controller currently issue an annual borrowing plan that is presented with the budget, setting forth the estimated borrowing needs and costs for the new fiscal year. The Commission believes such a report should be a mandatory part of the budget documents. The Commission also believes the current report should be accompanied by a summary of the specific plans for the repayment of all state debt not being provided for in the current and pending

---

[63] As pointed out in the Commission's Preliminary Report (page 38), other states place tax expenditure information within their budgets. In Massachusetts and Montana, one section of the Governor's budget is dedicated to detailing such tax preferences. In Michigan, the Department of Revenue provides tax expenditure information, which in 1992 showed that the dollar amount associated with income tax exemptions, deductions and credits actually exceeded the total income tax revenues the state collected.

[64] As previously noted, the World Wide Web address is: http://www.dof.ca.gov.

budgets, even though the financing instruments used for such debt repayment may be outside the budget process itself.

(c) *Summary of State Fiscal Resources and Transactions* As set forth in Part II above, only 70 per cent of state spending is done through the annual Budget Act. In addition, many state programs are funded through a combination of federal, state and local resources, yet aggregate information on federal and local spending and supporting revenues is not available in the Budget Act. Not only does the Budget Act not provide an all-inclusive summary of state revenues and spending—tax expenditures in particular—no other single source readily available to the public provides that information.

Summarizing all federal, state and local funding information in a single section of the Budget Act itself would allow the media, interested organizations and members of the public to assess the impact of state budget decisions on state-supported services and programs more knowledgeably. The total resources available to fund particular activities would be better understood, and the impact of specific funding decisions could be judged in the context of total program operations. The Commission, therefore, recommends that the state budget, as presented by the Governor, enacted by the Legislature and finally signed into law, contain a section summarizing all federal, state and local resources which are part of any state program.[65]

The Commission's Recommendation:

The Budget Act should include:

(a) a listing of all state tax expenditures,

(b) a statement of the State's overall fiscal condition, and

(c) a complete summary of state expenditures and revenues from all sources. (Statutory change)

Recommendation 13:
Distribute Clear And Simple Budget Information to the Public

The Governor's January budget proposal contains thousands of pages of detail. Yet, when approving the final budget or vetoing particular appropriations or pieces of budget bill language associated with appropriations, the Governor generally provides only the briefest explanation of the actions taken. Currently, the Department of Finance (DOF) and the Legislative Analyst's Office publish budget summaries. Although these documents are available to and understood by those

---

[65] This Recommendation is not intended to preclude action by the Governor and the Legislature to take care of unforeseen emergency situations that arise after the adoption of the budget. Such situations should be dealt with and reported in accordance with the procedures set forth in Recommendation 5 above.

who are close to the budget process, there is no single document widely available to the general public.

The Commission recommends that the DOF, in cooperation with the Legislative Analyst, be required by statute to prepare and issue a comprehensive final narrative budget summary explaining the budget's broad programs in simple language and in an easy-to-understand format within 60 days of the budget's adoption. That budget summary should provide a comprehensive description of the budget as enacted by the Legislature and signed by the Governor—as well as the reasons for the principal changes made by the Legislature to the Governor's original proposed budget.[66]

The availability of such information about the major activities of state government could help deepen the public's involvement in budget decision-making. As choices about future funding become clearer, the public's advocates would be better able to represent their interests.

> *Problem:*
> *The general public lacks adequate information about the adopted budget.*

The Commission further recommends that the State direct the DOF and the Legislative Analyst to prepare a short, easy-to-read budget "primer" to inform taxpayers how current dollars are spent. Taxpayers would better understand the connection between the taxes they pay and the programs their taxes fund. The public would become more aware of the budget process and be better able to hold legislators responsible for spending decisions.

The budget primer could be distributed separately with individual tax return forms sent out annually by the Franchise Tax Board (or possibly with voters' pamphlets in election years). Almost 12 million personal income tax returns are now filed in California each year. Since a large proportion of those are joint returns, a budget pamphlet included with all tax return forms mailed out by the Franchise Tax Board would reach the vast majority of California's more than 15 million registered voters, giving them convenient access to basic budget information.

Finally, the Commission suggests that the State needs to start preparing for the day when communication via the Internet and other electronic means will be the norm. At the local level, the City of Santa Monica is already receiving citizen input on its budget via the Internet.[67] Other jurisdictions are sure to follow suit.[68]

It is, of course, a long jump up from local cities, school districts and even counties to the State of California. Santa Monica has only about 100,000 residents and almost

[66] Presumably this summary would also be available on the World Wide Web sites maintained by DOF (http://www.dof.ca.gov) and the Legislature (http://www.assembly.ca.gov and http://www.sen.ca.gov).
[67] At http://pen.ci.santa-monica.ca.us/city/cityforms/budsug.html as of May 1, 1998. If not available, see the city's home page at http://pen.ci.santa-monica.ca.us for current information.
[68] The State may even take the lead here. The State's Commission on Local Governance for the 21st Century, now in formation, is instructed to report by June 1999 on, among other things, "criteria to increase citizen and community participation in city, county, and special district governments." Government Code Sec. 56302(c)(2).

one-half of its households are already connected to the Internet. City government can deal with citizen suggestions on an individual basis. On the other hand, the State has a population of more than 33 million. Any procedure for public budget input to the state budget process would necessarily require a way to organize incoming messages into a format both manageable and meaningful. To cite only one obvious problem, easy access to the Internet makes it a possible for a special interest group to generate enormous numbers of e-mail messages from its members on a particular issue. The State needs to have well-designed procedures ready for the day in the near future when Internet connections are standard features in most California households.[69]

Professor Genie N.L. Stowers at San Francisco State University published a short article, *Budgeting in Cyberspace,* on state and local government use of the Internet in connection with budgeting. Appearing on page 36 of the February 1998 issue of *Government Finance Review,* the article lists websites which should continue to provide current information on developments in this field.

The Commission's Recommendation:
A final budget summary in simple language should be prepared by the Department of Finance and the Legislative Analyst's Office for wide and immediate distribution, and an easy-to-read budget primer should be included in the taxpayer material mailed out annually to all taxpayers by the Franchise Tax Board. (Statutory change)

Recommendation 14:
Change to a Two-Year Budget

The State's budgetary system is oriented toward the annual fiscal year and lacks a long-term focus. Many of the largest programs are so complex that changes cannot be accomplished within a twelve-month timetable. A short-term focus can distort true costs and fail to alert lawmakers to imbalances between available revenues and program costs before they occur. The Commission recommends that the State adopt a two-year budget cycle, as is currently the practice in 20 other states. (See Appendix I.)

Each state department, particularly those responsible for the "Big Five" programs which account for most General Fund spending (as detailed in the General Fund section of Part II), should be required to review its primary mission, identify top priorities, estimate future costs of individual programs over a two-year period, and produce a cost containment plan that will consolidate, modernize and otherwise make program delivery systems more cost-efficient and productive. Reviewing

---

[69] Some groundwork is already being laid. A.B. 206 (Hertzberg), passed in 1997, added Sections 8330-32 to the Government Code. Those Sections require that state agencies which maintain sites on the World Wide Web must include on their Websites a procedure for citizens to make complaints to those agencies via the Internet.

> **Problem:**
> **The budget cycle is too short to allow for a proper long-term perspective and adequate public consideration of the complex issues to be decided.**

existing or proposed programs over a two-year period offers an opportunity for the Legislature to understand their costs and benefits more completely.

Obviously, a two-year budget would not eliminate the need for substantial expenditure adjustments during the second year. In a state as large and complex as California, changes will need to be made in the second half of the two-year budget span. Also, the newly elected legislators (and possibly Governor) may have different priorities after the elections in the even-numbered years of the budget adoptions. A second-year budget adjustment process, however, could focus on the items of necessary change and would not require the detailed evaluation of all state programs as is the case with the current annual budget cycle. The time saved should allow those involved in the budget process to give more attention to the long-range budget problems which the State constantly faces.

The Commission recognizes that in a two-year budget cycle the tendency will always exist for the Governor and the Legislature to postpone the pain of necessary budget reductions and/or revenue increases to the second year of the cycle, especially since budget adoptions would be in election years. Constant vigilance will be needed, particularly during periods of economic slowing, to prevent this tendency from turning the second year of the cycle into a deficit situation in violation of the balanced-budget principles set forth in Recommendations 1-5.

The Commission's Recommendation:
California should shift to a two-year state budget, to be adopted in even-numbered years. (Constitutional change)

Recommendation 15:
Include a Long-Term Strategic Spending Plan in the Budget Act

California's current budget process is largely the result of many short-term incremental decisions made without sufficient attention to long-term program needs and fiscal trends. Investments to meet future state objectives are debated within the narrow perspective of individual programs, rather than as part of a long-term process of setting overall priorities. Yet, ironically, the budget process is the most valuable opportunity California has each year to address the State's future requirements from a comprehensive perspective.

Repeatedly, the State has used short-term solutions to address its multi-billion-dollar revenue shortfalls and expenditure pressures. Those solutions often follow the path of least resistance by deferring major decisions and causing the underlying problems to grow. They compound future budget balancing problems and increase costs to taxpayers. Budget decision-makers will doubtless face major shortfalls in the future unless they implement programs to address the underlying problems in a long-term context.

Multi-billion-dollar spending programs require aggressive oversight and management. Fiscal oversight conducted solely through the annual budgeting process is not enough to control government expenses. Spending reductions or program restructuring often cannot be implemented in the budget year, since they take longer periods and often require federal approval. Managers of large spending programs often do not conduct adequate long-range fiscal planning, nor do they always develop effective plans to reduce costs or modify programs to ease future funding shortfalls.

> **Problem:**
> **The budget process is not sufficiently focused on long-term problems, solutions and costs.**

Throughout California's history, economic progress has followed deliberate efforts to link state spending priorities to economic growth. California's former preeminence in water, transportation and education are examples of such policies. Many people believe a strategy of long-term investment to meet the public needs of the State—such as schools, transportation, water and waste treatment—is critical to achieving continued economic growth. Some states formulate a "capital investment budget" to address separately those public activities designed to assist or foster economic growth.

For these reasons, the Commission recommends that the Budget Act include a long-term spending and public-investment plan with a clear statement of long-term state priorities. To facilitate the development and implementation of the long-term plan, the state budget documents should include five-year projections of expenditures and revenues.

The Commission further recommends that a five-year capital outlay plan be included in the state budget documents. Capital outlay needs—for construction of highways, hospitals, prisons, and so forth—are currently evaluated within the context of particular programs. For example, the capital investment in transportation is reviewed as part of the Cal-Trans budget, and the need for prisons is reviewed as part of the budget for the Department of Corrections.

In the past, the State had a single capital outlay plan and evaluated capital outlay projects across program lines—focusing investments on state objectives such as progressively monitored and prioritized educational, correctional, hospital and other service requirements and on population growth. But as federal funding became available for specific programs—for example, environmental protection and transportation—California began to narrow its capital outlay projects to match the availability of federal funding. Today, although much of this federal funding faces sharp reductions, the State has not reestablished its own overview program for capital funding. It needs to do so as soon as possible.[70]

Such long-term planning would provide an opportunity to rebuild consensus on the State's economic future. A long-term spending plan would also provide California with a comprehensive blueprint to use in reviewing current spending. Gauging future as well as current needs will help policymakers determine program priorities. In addition, a long-term spending plan would provide desirable continuity in an era of term limits and the resulting rapid turnover of legislators.

Understanding the long-term effects of budget decisions made to satisfy short-term needs is not a simple process. Although the Budget Act gives life to state activities for one year, it is important to look beyond those annual actions. Some short-run additional spending may save money in the long run; for example, preventive health care expenditures. Other programs also need a longer-term view. The importance of water resources to other development and the lead time for expansion of higher education facilities are only two of many examples showing the necessity to look ahead as the State's needs change and grow.

Legislation with substantial fiscal impact needs to be considered from this same perspective. However meritorious new programs may be, their ultimate cost must be taken into account and compared with the other demands on the State's limited resources. On the revenue side of the fiscal picture, it is just as essential that the State understand the long-term effects of tax policy changes. Some such changes, while difficult in the short term, may produce a fairer and more equitable tax system in the long term.

To provide the information necessary for proper fiscal decision-making, the Commission recommends that legislation be enacted to require that any bill which authorizes either substantial additional spending or substantial changes in revenue include an estimate of its fiscal implications over at least five years.

The Commission's Recommendation:

A long-term strategic spending plan (including a prioritized capital outlay program) should be included in the Budget Act. Five-year expenditure and revenue projections should be included in the state budget documents and in all legislation with substantial fiscal impacts. (Statutory change)

---

[70] S.B. 1069, introduced in 1997 by the Senate Committee on Budget and Fiscal Review and currently pending in the Assembly, requires that the Governor submit annually to the Legislature, as a supplement to the budget, a two-year and five-year capital outlay plan.

Accountability should be built into the state budget process.

California spends large sums on a wide range of programs, many of which lack clearly defined goals. Also, the State applies few measures of program effectiveness as it spends tax dollars. For this reason, program success or failure can be difficult to determine, and the average citizen has difficulty determining whether State programs are achieving their stated purposes and being operated in a cost-effective manner. In short, the state budget process lacks accountability.

The Commission makes the following recommendations to improve accountability:

16. Performance goals and objectives should be included in the state budget.

17. The state budget should also contain specific measures of program performance and effectiveness for all agencies and programs.

Recommendation 16:
Include Clear Program Objectives in the Budget Act

While the Governor's budget contains a "program objectives statement" for programs in most state departments, this often simply summarizes what the department or agency does, instead of explaining its goals and objectives. California's decision-makers need clear goals and objectives for current and future programs. The annual state budget process should reflect the State's priorities and policy agenda and should be consistent with the State's long-term goals and strategies.

> **Problem:**
> **The public has little understanding of the goals and objectives of many state programs.**

California's budget needs clear mission statements and long-range goals for all state programs. The commission recommends that the Governor's budget requests include a mission statement and explicit goals and objectives for each program. Such requests should also include a catalog of proposed services and program elements and the costs associated with each element. Those mission statements and goals and objectives should be carefully considered by the Legislature and should be part of the Budget Act when it is finally passed by the Legislature and signed by the Governor.

The Commission's Recommendation:
Performance and effectiveness objectives should be part of all state budget segments. (Statutory change)

Recommendation 17:
Include Program Performance Measures in the Budget Act

For many years, the Governor's Budget included performance measures for state agencies and departments. Those measurements gave an indication of how taxpayer dollars were being spent. However, such measures have not been included in the Governor's Budget since 1990-91.

The Commission recommends that specific measures of performance and effectiveness be returned to the state budget. The budget for each state agency and department should include, wherever possible, specific and quantifiable indicators to measure the success of a program and determine whether its intended beneficiaries actually benefited. These measures would help the State and the public to determine whether resources are being well-spent and to evaluate programs and the levels of taxation necessary to support them.

> **Problem:**
> **The state budget process does not include performance measures for many state programs and agencies.**

In fact, the Governor has implemented a pilot project on performance-based budgeting in four departments: the California Conservation Corps, the Department of Parks and Recreation, the Department of General Services and the Department of Consumer Affairs. The Governor anticipated that performance budgeting, along with quality performance efforts, could result in substantial cost savings, improved program performance, enhanced citizen satisfaction, and greater accountability.

These pilot projects focus on strategic planning, outcome measures for management accountability, and productivity benchmarks to measure progress toward strategic goals. The pilot departments enter into budget contracts with the Legislature to deliver specified outcomes for a specified level of resources. Managers are provided operational and administrative flexibility to achieve agreed-upon outcomes.

These pilot projects are still evolving; change comes slowly to a budget and management system built on control and procedures. They have raised questions regarding the value of certain state administrative rules and requirements. If these rules are reduced or eliminated for all state agencies, the result may be increased operational flexibility, greater reliance on performance objectives and measures and, hopefully, improved service throughout state government. The performance-based budgeting pilot projects have shown that performance measures can serve as agents of change, assisting state government to realign strategies, to improve human resource capabilities, and to enhance feedback and teamwork, thereby building better public understanding and support for state programs.

The Commission believes this project should be expanded to include all state government departments and agencies as soon as possible.[71]

The Commission's Recommendation:
The state budget should contain specific measures of program performance and effectiveness for all agencies and programs. (Statutory change)

Conclusion

The annual enactment of California's nation-sized budget presents an immense technical and political challenge to the Governor and the Legislature. To accomplish this critical task, a properly functioning state budget process is of great importance to the State's elected leadership, and to all Californians. Accordingly, California's fiscal decision-makers need to make use of the best possible practices in the preparation and adoption of the state budget.

As detailed above, the present state budget process is deficient in many important respects. The Recommendations detailed in Part III of this Final Report address those deficiencies. Prompt adoption of those Recommendations will greatly improve and strengthen the state budget process.

The size and complexity of California's state budget make it difficult for the average person to comprehend. The state budget process will never be an easy subject for civics classes. The recommendations presented in this Final report, however, will help make budget information more accessible and understandable for interested taxpayers and voters.

Fiscal information will become ever more available as we move into an era when the Internet and other communications media provide easier access to information technology, as well as the possibility of direct citizen input into the budget process. The proper use and dissemination of state budget information, pursuant to the Commission's Recommendations and taking advantage of new technologies, should deepen citizen understanding of and support for the State's budgetary decision-making.

---

[71] For a discussion of how performance-based budgeting might be applied to the State's health services, see the report, *A Shared Vision: A Practical Guide to the Design and Implementation of a Performance-Based Budget Model for California State Health Services,* California Citizen's Budget Commission (1997).

Part IV

Appendices

Appendix A

Tax Increase Voting Requirements

Majority vote required to pass revenue increase.

Alabama	Maryland	North Dakota
Alaska	Massachusetts	Ohio
Colorado*	Michigan	Pennsylvania
Connecticut	Minnesota	Rhode Island
Georgia	Missouri	South Carolina
Hawaii*	Montana	Tennessee
Idaho	Nebraska	Texas
Illinois	Nevada	Utah
Indiana	New Hampshire	Vermont
Iowa	New Jersey	Washington
Kentucky*	New Mexico	West Virginia
Kansas	New York	Wisconsin
Maine	North Carolina	Wyoming

3/5 vote required to pass revenue increase.

Mississippi	Delaware

2/3 vote required to pass revenue increase.

Arizona	Louisiana	Virginia*
California	Oregon	
Florida	South Dakota	

3/4 vote required to pass revenue increase.

Arkansas	Oklahoma

NOTES:

Colorado: All tax increases must be approved by a vote of the people.

Hawaii: Two-thirds of elected members are required if the general fund expenditure ceiling is exceeded; otherwise, a majority of elected members is required.

Kentucky: Majority voting for passage must include 2/5 of the members elected.

Virginia: Two-thirds of members voting for passage must include a majority of the members elected.

Source: National Association of State Budget Officers, Budget Processes in the States (1997).

Appendix B

States with Revenue and Spending Limits

State	Limitation
Alaska	Appropriations growth limited to growth of population and inflation.
Arizona	Appropriations limited to 7.23% of personal income.
California	Appropriations growth limited to growth of personal income and population.
Colorado	Appropriations growth limited to 6% of prior year's appropriation. General and Capital Fund revenues limited to growth of population and inflation.
Connecticut	Appropriations growth limited to greater of personal income growth or inflation.
Delaware	Appropriations limited to 98% of estimated income.
Florida	Revenue growth limited to five-year average of personal income growth.
Hawaii	Appropriations growth limited to three-year average of personal income growth.
Idaho	Appropriations limited to 5.33 % of personal income.
Iowa	Appropriations limited to 99% of adjusted general fund receipts.
Louisiana	Appropriations growth limited to per capita personal income growth.
Massachusetts	Revenue growth limited to growth in wages and salaries.
Michigan	Revenue limited to 9.49% of prior year's personal income.
Mississippi	Appropriations limited to 98% of projected revenue.
Missouri	Revenue limited to 5.64% of prior year's personal income.
Montana	Appropriations growth limited to personal income growth.
Nevada	Expenditure growth limited to growth of population and inflation.
New Jersey	Appropriations growth limited to personal income growth.
North Carolina	Appropriations limited to 7% of state personal income.
Oklahoma	Appropriations limited to 95% of certified revenue.
Oregon	Appropriations growth limited to personal income growth.
Rhode Island	Appropriations limited to 98% of projected revenue.
South Carolina	Appropriations growth limited to personal income growth.
Tennessee	Appropriations growth limited to personal income growth.
Texas	Appropriations growth limited to personal income growth.
Utah	Appropriations growth limited to growth in population, inflation and personal income.
Washington	State general fund expenditure growth limited to growth in population.

Source: National Association of State Budget Officers, *Budget Processes in the States* (1997).

Appendix C

Budget Adoption Calendar

State	Legislature Adopts Budget	State	Legislature Adopts Budget
Alabama	Feb./May	Nebraska	April
Alaska	May	Nevada	June
Arizona	Jan./April	New Hampshire	May
Arkansas	Jan./April	New Jersey	June
California	June 15	New Mexico	Feb./March
Colorado	May	New York	March
Connecticut	June/May	North Carolina	June
Delaware	June 30	North Dakota	Jan./April
Florida	April/May	Ohio	June
Georgia	March	Oklahoma	May
Hawaii	April	Oregon	Jan./June
Idaho	March	Pennsylvania	June
Illinois	May	Rhode Island	June
Indiana	April	South Carolina	June
Iowa	April/May	South Dakota	March
Kansas	May	Tennessee	April/May
Kentucky	April	Texas	May
Louisiana	June	Utah	February
Maine	June	Vermont	May
Maryland	April	Virginia	March/April
Massachusetts	June	Washington	April/May
Michigan	July	West Virginia	March
Minnesota	May	Wisconsin	June/July
Missouri	April/May	Wyoming	March
Montana	April		

Source: National Association of State Budget Officers, *Budget Processes in the States* (1997).

Appendix D

Gubernatorial Veto

States with Line-Item Veto

Alaska	Kentucky*	Ohio*
Arizona	Louisiana	Oklahoma
Arkansas	Maine	Oregon
California	Massachusetts	Pennsylvania
Colorado	Michigan	South Carolina
Connecticut	Minnesota	South Dakota
Delaware	Mississippi	Tennessee
Florida	Missouri	Texas
Georgia	Montana	Utah
Hawaii	Nebraska	Virginia
Idaho	New Jersey	Washington
Illinois*	New Mexico	West Virginia
Iowa	New York*	Wisconsin
Kansas	North Dakota	Wyoming

States without Line-Item Veto

Alabama*	Nevada	Rhode Island
Indiana	New Hampshire	Vermont
Maryland	North Carolina	

NOTES:

Alabama: As long as the Legislature is in session, the Governor can return a bill without limit for recommended amendments as to amount and language.

Illinois: The Governor can veto appropriation items entirely (item veto) or merely reduce an item of appropriation to a lesser amount (reduction veto). If the Governor reduces an item of appropriation, the remaining items in the bill are not affected and can become law immediately. The Governor can also veto substantive or appropriation bills entirely (veto) or merely make changes to them (amendatory veto). Changes can include removing selected words or changing the meaning of words. If the Governor makes amendatory language changes to an appropriation bill, the entire bill, including all other appropriation items, is held up until the Legislature considers the Governor's changes.

Kentucky: Constitutional authority is unclear because issue has not been litigated.

New York: Any appropriation added to the Governor's budget by the Legislature is subject to line-item veto.

Ohio: Line-item veto in appropriation act only.

Source: National Association of State Budget Officers, *Budget Processes in the States* (1997).

Appendix E

Budgeting Procedures

Budget Uses GAAP

Alaska	Michigan	Tennessee
Arkansas	Mississippi	Utah
Colorado	Montana	Washington
Connecticut	New Jersey	Wyoming
Georgia	New York	
Iowa	Rhode Island	

Budget Does Not Use GAAP

Alabama	Maine	Oklahoma
Arizona	Maryland	Oregon
Delaware	Massachusetts	South Carolina
Florida	Minnesota	South Dakota
Hawaii	Missouri	Texas
Idaho	Nebraska	Vermont
Illinois	Nevada	Virginia
Indiana	New Hampshire	West Virginia
Kansas	New Mexico	Wisconsin
Kentucky	North Carolina	
Louisiana	North Dakota	

Special Cases

California — The state prepares the annual budget on a legal basis. These budget amounts, on a summary level, are then converted to reflect a GAAP basis.

Ohio — Separate GAAP financial statements are published annually.

Pennsylvania — Uses program budgets: Separate GAAP financial statements are published annually but not in the budget.

Source: National Association of State Budget Officers, *Budget Processes in the States* (1997).

Appendix F

Balanced Budget Requirements

Governor must submit balanced budget.

Alabama	Alaska	Arizona	Arkansas
California	Colorado	Connecticut	Delaware
Florida	Georgia	Hawaii	Illinois
Iowa	Kansas	Kentucky	Louisiana
Maine	Maryland	Massachusetts	Michigan
Minnesota	Mississippi	Missouri	Montana
Nebraska	Nevada	New Hampshire	New Jersey
New Mexico	New York	North Carolina	North Dakota
Ohio	Oklahoma	Oregon	Pennsylvania
Rhode Island	South Carolina	South Dakota	Tennessee
Utah	Washington	Wisconsin	Wyoming

Legislature must pass balanced budget.

Alabama	Alaska	Arizona	Arkansas
Colorado	Connecticut	Delaware	Florida
Georgia	Idaho*	Illinois	Iowa
Kansas	Kentucky	Louisiana	Maine
Maryland	Massachusetts	Michigan	Minnesota
Mississippi	Montana	Nebraska	Nevada
New Jersey	New Mexico	North Carolina	North Dakota
Ohio	Oklahoma*	Oregon	Rhode Island
South Carolina	South Dakota	Tennessee	Texas
Utah	West Virginia	Wisconsin	Wyoming

Governor must sign balanced budget.

Alaska	Arizona	Arkansas	Colorado
Connecticut	Delaware	Florida	Georgia
Hawaii	Kentucky	Louisiana	Maine
Massachusetts	Michigan	Minnesota	Missouri
Nevada	New Jersey	New Mexico	New York*
North Dakota	Ohio	Oklahoma*	Oregon
Pennsylvania	Rhode Island	South Carolina	South Dakota
Tennessee	Texas	West Virginia	Wisconsin

No balanced-budget requirements by statute or constitution.

Indiana	Vermont	Virginia*

NOTES:

Idaho: Although the constitution requires that the Legislature pass a balanced budget, there have been years when they over-appropriated the revenue estimate. The Governor, as the chief budget officer of the State, ensures that expenditures do not exceed revenues.

New York: The Governor is not technically required to sign a balanced budget, but the Governor, legislative leaders and the Comptroller must certify that the budget is in balance in order to meet lending requirements.

Oklahoma: The Legislature could pass and the Governor could sign a budget in which appropriations exceed cash and estimated revenues, but constitutional and statutory provisions would reduce appropriations and balance the budget.

Virginia: Balance requirements apply only to budget execution. The Governor is required to ensure that actual expenditures do not exceed actual revenues.

Source: National Association of State Budget Officers, *Budget Processes in the States* (1997).

Appendix G

Gubernatorial Authority to Reduce Enacted Budget

Governor may reduce budget without legislative approval.
(Restrictions noted.)

Arkansas*	Missouri	Tennessee
Colorado	New Jersey	Texas
Georgia*	New York*	Virginia*
Hawaii*	North Carolina*	West Virginia*
Idaho*	Ohio	Wisconsin*
Indiana	Oklahoma*	Wyoming
Maryland*	Pennsylvania*	
Massachusetts	Rhode Island	

Governor can reduce across the board only.
(Legislative approval required except as noted.)

Alabama	Maine	South Carolina*
Iowa	Mississippi	Utah*
Kansas*	North Dakota	Washington

Maximum reduction specified.
(Legislative approval required except as noted.)

Connecticut	Minnesota	Oregon
Florida*	Montana*	
Louisiana	Nevada	

Governor may not reduce budget without legislative approval.

Alaska	Illinois	New Hampshire
Arizona	Kentucky	New Mexico
California	Michigan*	South Dakota
Delaware	Nebraska	Vermont*

NOTES:

Arkansas: The Governor and chief fiscal officer of the State have the authority to reduce general revenue funding to agencies should shortfalls occur in revenue collections. Legislative approval not required.

Florida: The elected cabinet (Administrative Commission) for the Executive Branch and the Chief Justice of the Supreme Court for the Judicial Branch are authorized to resolve deficits of less than $300 million. Deficits of more than $300 million must be resolved by the Legislature.

Georgia: The Governor, during the first six months of a fiscal year in which the current revenue estimate on which appropriations are based is expected to exceed actual revenues, is authorized to require state agencies to reserve such appropriations as specified by the Governor for budget reductions to be recommended to the General Assembly at its next regular session.

Hawaii: The Governor's authority to reorganize, expand and reduce budgets can be exercised only pursuant to existing statutes.

Idaho: The Governor's authority to reduce budgets is temporary. The State Board of Examiners (Governor, Attorney General, and Secretary of State) has permanent appropriation reduction authority.

Kansas: Legislative approval not required.

Maine: Legislative approval not required.

Maryland: With the approval of the Board of Public Works, the Governor may reduce by not more than 25% any appropriation that the Governor considers unnecessary. The Governor may not, however, reduce an appropriation (a) to the legislative or judicial branches of government; (b) for the payment of principal and interest on state debt; (c) for the funding for public schools (K-12); or (d) for the salary of a public officer during the term of office.

Michigan: Executive branch authority to make budget reductions is restricted by statutory and constitutional limitations requiring approval of the reductions by both House and Senate Appropriations Committees.

Montana: Additional restrictions on budget reductions exclude principal and interest on state debt, legislative and judicial branches, school equalization aid and salaries of elected officials.

New York: May reduce budget without approval for state operations. Only restriction is reductions in aid to localities cannot be made without legislative approval.

North Carolina: Except certain block grants.

Oklahoma: Would require agreement of agency governing boards and/or CEO.

Pennsylvania: The Governor may reduce budgets selectively. Before lapsing current year grant and subsidy money, the Governor must provide 10-day prior notice and the reasons for so doing.

South Carolina: The Budget and Control Board can authorize an across-the-board agency reduction when there is a revenue shortfall. When in session, the General Assembly has five statewide session days to take action to prevent the reduction.

Utah: There are some restrictions. For example, debt services cannot be cut.

Vermont: Reductions based on revenue shortfalls of greater than 1% require legislative approval.

Virginia: Cannot reduce appropriations, but can withhold allotments.

West Virginia: The Governor can reduce expenditures but not appropriations. Public education has priority.

Wisconsin: Cannot reduce appropriations, but can withhold allotments.

Source: National Association of State Budget Officers, *Budget Processes in the States* (1997).

Appendix H

Vote Required to Pass the Budget

Majority of those present required to pass budget.

Alabama	Louisiana	North Dakota
Alaska*	Maine*	Ohio
Arizona	Massachusetts	Oregon
Connecticut	Michigan	South Carolina
Delaware	Montana	Tennessee
Florida	Nevada	Texas
Georgia	New Hampshire	Utah
Idaho	New Jersey	Vermont
Indiana	New Mexico	Washington
Iowa	New York	Wisconsin
Kansas	North Carolina	Wyoming

Majority of elected members required to pass budget

Colorado	Minnesota	Pennsylvania
Hawaii*	Mississippi*	South Dakota*
Illinois*	Missouri	Virginia
Kentucky	Oklahoma	West Virginia
Maryland		

Other

Arkansas*	Nebraska*	Rhode Island*
California*		

NOTES:

Alaska: A simple majority is required to pass the budget. A 3/4 majority is required for withdrawals from the budget reserve fund to balance revenues and expenditures.

Arkansas: A majority is required for education, highways and confederate pensions; 3/4 of the elected is required on all others.

California: 2/3 of the elected members.

Hawaii: If General Fund expenditure ceiling is exceeded, two-thirds vote required; otherwise majority of elected members.

Illinois: A majority vote in each house is required to pass the budget until June 1. After that date, the required vote increases to 3/5 majority.

Maine: For the first time in recent history, the Legislature enacted the 1997-98 budget on a simple majority vote in both Houses. The 118th Maine Legislature's first regular session was then adjourned sine die, the first special session was convened and the normal 90-day waiting period for non-emergency bills began (on approximately 3/27/97).

Mississippi: Agency Appropriations Bill majority elected, unless a bill is considered a donation. In this case, Joint Rule 66 requires 2/3 of the elected (i.e., donation to the Mississippi Burn Center).

Nebraska: Main budget bills typically have the "e" (emergency) clause attached, thus requiring 2/3 vote. (The "e" clause is necessary to be operative by the beginning of the fiscal year.) Otherwise 3/5 of the elected members.

Rhode Island: 2/3 of both houses.

South Dakota: 2/3 majority is required for individual spending bills.

Source: National Conference of State Legislatures, *Legislative Budget Procedures in the States and Territories* (1998).

Appendix I

Budget Cycles

Annual Budget Cycle

Alabama	Iowa	Oklahoma
Alaska	Louisiana	Pennsylvania
California	Maryland	Rhode Island
Colorado	Massachusetts	South Carolina
Delaware	Michigan	South Dakota
Florida	Mississippi	Tennessee
Georgia	New Jersey	Utah
Idaho	New Mexico	Vermont
Illinois	New York	West Virginia

Biennial Budget Cycle

Arkansas	Montana	Oregon
Connecticut	Nebraska	Texas
Hawaii	Nevada	Virginia
Indiana	New Hampshire	Washington
Kentucky	North Carolina	Wisconsin
Maine	North Dakota	Wyoming
Minnesota	Ohio	

Special Cases

Arizona   Agencies are divided into major budget units and other budget units. Major budget units submit annual budget requests. Other budget units submit biennial budget requests. Beginning with the fiscal years 2000 – 2001 biennium, all agencies will be on a biennial budget cycle.

Kansas   Twenty agencies are on a biennial budget cycle. The rest are on an annual cycle.

Missouri   There is constitutional authority to do annual and biennial budgeting. Beginning in fiscal year 1994, the operating budget has been annual while the capital budget has been biennial.

Source: National Association of State Budget Officers, *Budget Processes in the States* (1997).

Appendix J

Proposed Constitutional and Statutory Changes to Implement the Recommendations of the Commission

Recommendation No. 1: All future state budgets—as presented by the Governor, passed by the Legislature and signed by the Governor—should be required to have a balanced General Fund. Budgeted General Fund expenditures should not exceed estimated revenues for the budget cycle. *(Constitutional change)*

Proposed Constitutional Amendment:
(New Subsection (f) to be added to Section 12 of Article IV)

(f) The total of all expenditures that are authorized to be made from the General Fund of the State by the Budget Act for the ensuing fiscal period for which the Budget Act is adopted, combined with the total of all General Fund reserves required under Subsection (g) for that fiscal period and any deficit in the General Fund remaining from preceding fiscal periods, may not exceed the total of all revenues and other resources, including reserves for prior years, that are estimated to be available to the State for General Fund purposes for that ensuing fiscal period. The total amount of those expenditures, revenues, reserves, deficit and other resources, as of the date of the Budget Act, shall be set forth expressly in that Act. The total resources shall not include borrowed amounts other than funds borrowed in accordance with the provisions of Sections 1, 1.1 and 1.2 of Article XVI.

Recommendation No. 2: External borrowing to finance a General Fund deficit should be prohibited, except to meet legitimate cash flow needs within the current and immediately succeeding budget year. Rollover of such short-term debt to any later budget year should occur only in the event of defined emergency circumstances voted by a 60% majority of both houses of the Legislature. *(Constitutional change)*

Proposed Constitutional Amendment:
(New Section 1.1 to be added to Article XVI)

Section 1.1 (a) Except as to any indebtedness approved by the voters pursuant to Section 1, during any annual fiscal period for which a budget bill is to be, or has been enacted, the legislature shall not in any manner create any debt or debts, or liabilities, unless they are repaid during that same or the immediately succeeding annual fiscal period. For purposes of this section, "debt or debts, or liability or liabilities" includes an obligation for which an appropriation is made from anticipated funds, but does not include borrowing between state funds.

(b) Notwithstanding paragraph (a), by enactment of a bill describing the reasons for the delay in retiring the debt and passed in each house by a 60% majority roll-call vote entered in the journal, the legislature may, during recessionary fiscal years [as defined by a statute passed pursuant to paragraph 12(g)(4) of Article IV], roll over short-term debt to the next fiscal year.

Recommendation No. 3: Long-term debt should be limited to capital items. *(Constitutional change)*

Proposed Constitutional Amendment:
(New Section 1.2 to be added to Article XVI)

Section 1.2 No long-term debt or liability shall be created or incurred unless it is specifically authorized for covering the costs of capital projects (including the cost of designing and equipping the capital projects and the financing costs involved). As used in this section, "long-term debt or liability" is defined as a debt or liability which is not repaid in full during the same fiscal year in which it is created or incurred or during the five fiscal years immediately following.

Recommendation No. 4:   Off-budget state expenditures and borrowing should be constitutionally prohibited. *(Constitutional change)*

Proposed Constitutional Amendment:
(New Subsection 12(i) to be added to Article IV)

(i) The Budget Act shall include all appropriations for state expenditures in the fiscal period covered by the act. The State may not expend any funds for any purpose for any fiscal period unless the appropriation authorizing that expenditure is made in a Budget Act or in an amendment to a Budget Act.

Recommendation No. 5:   During both legislative sessions and interim periods, the Joint Legislative Budget Committee should have the responsibility of recommending any legislative actions needed to keep the budget in balance. In the absence of corrective action by the Legislature, the Governor should have the authority to make such expenditure reductions as are needed to maintain the balance. *(Statutory change)*

Proposed Statutory Change:
(New Government Code Section)

Section 13309.
(a) The Director of Finance and the Legislative Analyst shall both monitor expenditures and revenues during the term of each budget and issue periodic reports regarding whether the expenditures are expected to exceed anticipated revenues. The Joint Legislative Budget Committee shall review those reports and may recommend changes in the Budget Act to keep the budget in balance.
(b) In the event that a potential budgetary deficit is reported and remedial legislation is not enacted, the Governor may, after 30 days' written notice to the Joint Legislative Budget Committee, adjust expenditures by executive order in an

amount sufficient to eliminate the potential deficit. Within 30 days after such an executive order, the Legislature may, by a two-thirds roll-call vote entered in the journal of each house, override the Governor's executive order.

Recommendation No. 6: The state budget should be enacted by a simple majority vote of the two houses of the Legislature. *(Constitutional change)*

Proposed Constitutional Amendment:
*(Amendment to Subsection 12(d) of Article IV. **Changes in bold**)*

(d) No bill except the budget bill may contain more than one item of appropriation, and that for one certain, expressed purpose. Appropriations from the General Fund of the State, except appropriations for the public schools **or appropriations made in the Budget Act or amendments thereto,** are void unless passed in each house by roll-call vote entered in the journal, two-thirds of the membership concurring.

Recommendation No. 7: Budget implementation bills should be treated as part of the state budget: adopted by majority vote, subject to the line-item veto and not limited by the single-subject rule. *(Constitutional change)*

Proposed Constitutional Amendment:
(New Subsection 9(b) to be added to Article IV)

(b) (1) One or more statutes may be enacted for the period covered by each budget bill that embraces more than one subject if the statute makes changes in law that are necessary to the implementation of the appropriations authorized in that budget bill, if that fact is expressed in the title of the bill enacting the statute, and if that bill is presented to the Governor at the same time as the budget bill.

(2) If the Governor reduces or eliminates an appropriation from the budget bill, the Governor may eliminate that part of any statute enacted pursuant to this subsection which makes changes in law necessary to the implementation of that appropriation while approving other provisions of that statute. The Governor may not, however, eliminate provisions of the statute that are unrelated to the appropriations reduced or eliminated by the Governor from the budget bill. Any part of a statute eliminated by the Governor pursuant to this paragraph shall be separately reconsidered and may be passed over the Governor's veto in the same manner as bills.

(3) If the statute makes a substantive change in law that is not necessary to the implementation of one or more of the appropriations in the budget bill, the section of the bill containing that change is void. The Governor, while approving other sections of the bill, may eliminate one or more sections that he or she determines not to be necessary to the implementation of one or more appropriations in the budget bill. Any section of the bill eliminated by the Governor pursuant to such a determination shall be separately reconsidered and may be passed over the Governor's veto in the same manner as bills.

Recommendation No. 8: Tax expenditures should be created, modified or repealed in accordance with the same vote requirement: a majority vote of the Legislature. *(Constitutional change)*

Proposed Constitutional Amendment:

(Amendment to be made to Section 3 of Article XIII A. **Changes in bold***)*

Section 3. **(a)** From and after the effective date of this article, any changes in state taxes enacted for the purpose of increasing revenues collected pursuant thereto whether by increased rates or changes in methods of computation must be imposed by an Act passed by not less than two-thirds of all members elected to each of the two houses of the Legislature, except that no new *ad valorem* taxes on real property, or sales or transaction taxes on the sales of real property may be imposed.

(b) Notwithstanding the provisions of subsection (a), a bill creating, amending or repealing any tax expenditure, as defined in subsection (c), shall be passed by the vote of a majority of all members elected to each of the two houses of the Legislature.

(c) For purposes of this Section, a "tax expenditure" is:

(1) Any exclusion or exemption from any tax.

(2) Any deduction from any amount subject to any tax.

(3) Any credit against any tax.

(4) Any preferential treatment of any item subject to any tax.

(5) Any preferential tax rate.

(6) Any deferral of any tax.

Recommendation No. 9: In even-numbered years, the legislative session should have a period, beginning June 1 and ending with the passage of the Budget Act, when adoption of the budget would be the only order of business. *(Constitutional change)*

Proposed Constitutional Amendment:

(Amendment to be made to Subsection 12 (c) of Article IV. **Changes in bold***)*

(c) The budget shall be accompanied by a budget bill itemizing recommended expenditures. The bill shall be introduced immediately in each house by the persons chairing the committees that consider appropriations. **From June 1 until the budget bill is enacted, except by unanimous consent of both houses, no other bill may be heard or acted on by committee or either house.** The Legislature shall pass the budget bill by midnight on June 15 of each year. Until the budget bill has been enacted, the Legislature shall not send to the Governor for consideration any bill appropriating funds for expenditure during the fiscal year for which the budget bill is to be enacted, except emergency bills recommended by the Governor or appropriations for the salaries and expenses of the Legislature.

Recommendation No. 10: In every budget cycle, the Joint Legislative Budget Committee should review and issue a report on the fiscal impact of all constitutional and statutory expenditure and revenue constraints on the state budget process. On a quadrennial basis, an independent body should be created to conduct a similar review (to include all continuing appropriations and special funds) and recommend appropriate modifications of those constraints to the Legislature. The Legislature should be authorized, acting by majority vote, to submit to a vote of the people such of those recommendations as involve constitutional amendments. *(Constitutional and statutory changes)*

Proposed Constitutional Amendment:
(New Subsection (j) to be added to Section 12 of Article IV)

(j) (1) During calendar year 2004, and every four years thereafter, an independent board shall review and report on the cumulative fiscal impacts of all constitutional and statutory expenditure and revenue constraints affecting the state budget process. This report may include proposed constitutional and statutory amendments. The Legislature shall implement this subdivision by statute.

(2) Notwithstanding Section 1 of Article XVIII, the Legislature may propose an amendment to the Constitution, by roll-call vote entered in the journal, a majority of the membership of each house concurring, to implement one or more proposals submitted pursuant to subparagraph (1).

Proposed Statutory Amendments:
(New Sections of the Government Code)

Section 9143.7 At the conclusion of every budget cycle, the committee shall review and report on the cumulative fiscal impacts of all constitutional and statutory expenditure and revenue constraints affecting the state budget process, which may include recommended constitutional and statutory changes. The Legislative Analyst shall assist the committee in this task.

Section 8275

(a) Purpose The Legislature finds and declares that California's state budget process is greatly limited by numerous constitutional and statutory constraints on its expenditures and revenue procedures and that these constraints should be regularly reviewed and analyzed in light of the state's current needs and responsibilities.

(b) Creation There is created in state government on a quadrennial basis the California State Budget Commission.

(c) Membership The Commission shall consist of ___ members, as follows:

___ members appointed by the Governor. No more than ___ members may be registered with the same political party.

___ members appointed by the Assembly Committee on Rules. No more than ___ members may be registered with the same political party. ___ member(s) shall be appointed in consultation with the Assembly Minority Caucus.

___members appointed by the Senate Committee on Rules. No more than ___ members may be registered with the same political party. ___ member(s) shall be appointed in consultation with the Senate Minority Caucus.

The Chief Justice of California, or her or his designee.

(d) Personnel & Assistance

The Governor shall select one of the members as the chair of the commission.

The commission may appoint an executive secretary and fix her or his compensation in accordance with law. The commission may employ and fix the compensation, in accordance with law, of any professional, clerical and other assistants that may be necessary.

The Legislative Counsel, Legislative Analyst, State Auditor and the Department of Finance shall assist the commission in the performance of its duties.

(e) Duties The commission shall assist the Governor and the Legislature by:

Examining the state budget process and evaluating the extent to which the budget process serves the future needs of the state.

Examining and evaluating the current configuration of state and local government duties, responsibilities and priorities and the fiscal relations of state and local governments.

Examining and evaluating the types of services delivered, the desired program outcomes, and the methods of performance measurement.

(f) Reports The commission shall begin meeting in July of the first year of each new gubernatorial term and shall submit a report to the Governor and the Legislature no later than the end of the following year. The report shall set forth the commission's findings and recommendations with respect to its mandate. The commission may submit interim reports before that date whenever it makes a finding and recommendation on a specific topic.

(g) Powers In carrying out its duties and responsibilities, the commission shall have the following powers:

To meet at such times and places as it may deem proper. The commission is a state body subject to the provisions of the Bagley-Keene Open Meeting Act [Article 9 (commencing with Section 11120) of Chapter 1 of Part 1 of Division 3].

To issue subpoenas to compel the attendance of witnesses and the production of books, records, papers, accounts, reports and other documents.

To administer oaths.

To contract, as it deems necessary, for the rendition of services, facilities, studies and reports to the commission as will best assist it to carry out its duties and responsibilities.

To cooperate with and to secure the cooperation of county, city and other local agencies in investigating any matter within the scope of its duties and responsibilities.

To secure directly from every state and local department, agency or instrumentality full cooperation, access to its records and access to any information, suggestions, estimates, date and statistics that it may have available.

To do any and all things necessary or convenient to enable it fully and adequately to perform its duties and to exercise the powers expressly granted to it.

Recommendation No. 11: California should have a unified and comprehensive state budget process. All projected expenditures, revenues and tax expenditures (including all subventions to and transfers from other levels of government) should be included in that process. *(Constitutional change)*

Proposed Constitutional Amendment:
(New Subsection (h) to be added to Section 12 of Article IV)

(h) The Budget Act should be a comprehensive statement of all state resources, expenditures and obligations. The Budget Act should include, but not be limited to, all estimated expenditures and revenues for the General Fund and all special funds, all estimated subventions to and transfers from other levels of government, all estimated tax expenditures (as defined by statute), an estimate of the accumulated surplus or deficit, and all long and short-term state borrowing.

Recommendation No. 12: The Budget Act should include:
(a) a listing of all state tax expenditures,
(b) a statement of the State's overall fiscal condition, and
(c) a complete summary of state expenditures and revenues from all sources.
(Statutory change)

Proposed Statutory Amendment:
(New Section to be added to the Government Code)

Section 13337.1
(a) The Budget Act shall contain a separate section summarizing in concise, everyday language all estimated expenditures and revenues for the General Fund and all special funds (including all subventions to and transfers from other levels of government and all tax expenditures).

(b)   The Budget Act shall contain a separate section setting forth in concise, everyday language a statement of the state's overall fiscal condition (including an estimate of the total accumulated surplus or deficit and a summary of all short and long-term borrowing with the associated debt service expenses). The documentation accompanying the Budget Act shall include a borrowing plan setting forth the estimated borrowing needs and costs for the new budget cycle and a summary of the repayment plans for all state debt not provided for in the current and pending budget cycles.

(c)   The Budget Act shall contain a separate section in concise, everyday language listing all tax expenditures and including, for each item, the estimated revenue loss and number of taxpayers affected.

(d)   For purposes of this subdivision, a "tax expenditure" is:

(1)   Any exclusion or exemption from any tax.

(2)   Any deduction from any amount subject to any tax.

(3)   Any credit against any tax.

(4)   Any preferential treatment of any item subject to any tax.

(5)   Any preferential tax rate.

(6)   Any deferral of any tax.

Recommendation No. 13: A final budget summary in simple language should be prepared by the Department of Finance and the Legislative Analyst's Office for wide and immediate distribution, and an easy-to-read budget primer should be included in the taxpayer material mailed out annually to all taxpayers by the Franchise Tax Board. *(Statutory change)*

Proposed Statutory Amendment:
(New Section to be added to the Government Code)

Section 13337.2 As soon as possible after final enactment of the Budget Act, the Department of Finance and the Legislative Analyst shall prepare a summary of the budget in concise, everyday language for immediate wide distribution to the media and the public. The Department and the Analyst shall also prepare an easy-to-read budget primer for inclusion with the personal income tax forms distributed by the Franchise Tax Board pursuant to Article 3 (commencing with Section 19581) of Chapter 7 of Part 10.2 of Division 2 of the Revenue and Taxation Code.

Recommendation No. 14: California should shift to a two-year state budget, to be adopted in even-numbered years. *(Constitutional change)*

Proposed Constitutional Amendments:
(Subsection 12(a) of Article IV to be amended to read as follows.)

Section 12 (a)

(1) Within the first 10 days of each even-numbered year, the Governor shall submit to the Legislature, with an explanatory message, a budget for the two-year fiscal period commencing on the ensuing July 1, containing itemized statements for recommended state expenditures and estimated state revenues. If recommended expenditures exceed estimated revenues, the Governor shall recommend the sources from which the additional revenues should be provided.

(2) (A) No later than February 1 of each odd-numbered calendar year, the Governor shall submit to the Legislature a budget rebalancing plan containing recommendations for adjustment in expenditures or revenues, or other changes, as necessary to maintain the balance required by subdivision (f) throughout the two-year period for which the budget bill was enacted. The plan shall be accompanied, as appropriate, by a budget rebalancing bill itemizing those adjustments or other necessary changes. The bill shall be introduced immediately in each house by the persons chairing the committees that consider the budget.

(B) If the Governor determines that no adjustments are necessary for the purpose described in paragraph (A), he or she shall submit to the Legislature by February 1 a report updating, for the current fiscal period, the totals of expenditures, reserves, deficits and revenues and other resources identified for that fiscal period pursuant to subdivision (f).

Conforming changes would also need to be made to Subdivision 12(c) of Article IV (budget bill procedure), Article XIII B (spending limits), Section 8 of Article XVI (school financing guarantees) and other affected sections of the Constitution.

Proposed Statutory Amendments:

In addition, numerous conforming changes would need to be made to the Government Code, the Revenue and Taxation Code and various other affected codes.

Recommendation No. 15: A long-term strategic spending plan (including a prioritized capital outlay program) should be included in the Budget Act. Five-year expenditure and revenue projections should be included in the state budget documents and in all legislation with substantial fiscal impacts. *(Statutory change)*

Proposed Statutory Amendment:
(New Subsection to be added to the Government Code)

Section 13337.1 (b)
(1) The Budget Act shall include a long-term strategic spending plan that includes a prioritized investment and capital outlay program.

(2) Five-year expenditure and revenue projections should be included in the state budget documentation and should be provided with all legislation having a substantial fiscal impact.

Recommendation No. 16: Performance and effectiveness objectives should be part of all state budget segments. *(Statutory change)*

Recommendation No. 17: The state budget should contain specific measures of program performance and effectiveness for all agencies and programs. *(Statutory change)*

Proposed Statutory Amendment:
(New Subsection to be added to proposed Government Code Section 13337.1)

(e) The proposed budget submitted by the Governor and the Budget Act, as finally enacted, shall set forth performance and effectiveness objectives, as well as specific measures of program performance and effectiveness, wherever feasible, for each agency and program to be funded by the Budget Act.

Appendix K

Bibliography

I. Regular Periodicals and Reports

The California Budget Project, *Budget Watch* (semi-monthly)

California Taxpayers' Association, *Cal-Tax Digest* (monthly), *Cal-Tax News* (semi-monthly through 1995)

Governing Magazine, *State & Local Sourcebook* (annual supplement)

State of California:

Assembly Budget Committee and Senate Committee on Budget and Fiscal Review, *Overview of Budget Bill* (annual)

Auditor General, *Annual State Financial Report*

Department of Finance (all annual)

Governor's Budget

Governor's Budget Summary

May Revision

Final Change Book

Final Budget Summary

Tax Expenditure Report

Capital Outlay and Infrastructure Report

Economic Report of the Governor

Franchise Tax Board, *Annual Report*

Legislative Analyst's Office (annual except as noted):

Analysis of the Budget Bill

Annual Report to the Joint Legislative Budget Committee

Perspectives and Issues

California Spending Plan

California's Fiscal Outlook

California Update (monthly)

Office of the State Controller, *Comprehensive Annual Financial Report*

State Board of Equalization, *Annual Report*

State Public Works Board & State Treasurer, *Official Statements on State Bond Issuances*

II. Articles, Books, Pamphlets and Reports

Briffault, Richard, *Balancing Acts: The Reality Behind State Balanced Budget Requirements,* Twentieth Century Fund Report (1996)

Cain, Bruce E. and Roger G. Noll (editors), *Constitutional Reform In California: Making State Government More Effective and Responsive, Section V,* Institute of Governmental Studies Press, University of California, Berkeley (1995)

The California Budget Project, *State and Local Government Finance in California: A Primer* (July 1996)

California Business-Higher Education Forum, *California Fiscal Reform: A Plan for Action, Recommendations and Summary* (June 1994)

California Constitution Revision Commission, *Final Report and Recommendations to the Governor and the Legislature,* pages 33-44 (1996)

California Council for Environmental and Economic Balance, *List of Concepts for Discussion for Government Efficiency and Accountability Reforms* (May 30, 1994)

Carroll, Stephen J., Kevin F. McCarthy and Mitchell Wade, "California's Looming Budget Crisis," *RAND Research Review Vol. XVIII, No. 2* (Fall 1994)

Forsythe, Dall W., *Memos to the Governor: An Introduction to State Budgeting,* Georgetown University Press (1997)

Hartley, James et al. "Reform During Crisis: The Transformation of California's Fiscal System During the Great Depression," *Journal of Economic History* (September 1996)

Hill, Elizabeth G., Legislative Analyst, *Analysis of the 1991-92 Tax Expenditure Budget,* Legislative Analyst's Office (May 1991)

Hill, Elizabeth G., Legislative Analyst, *California's Tax Structure,* Presentation to the Senate Revenue and Taxation Committee (February 15, 1995)

Little Hoover Commission, *State Fiscal Condition Report, Executive Summary* (March 1995)

Kiewiet, D. Roderick, *Constitutional Limitations on Indebtedness: The Case of California,* California Institute of Technology (June 1995)

LaVally, Rebecca and Tim Fong, *The History of State Deficits in California*, Senate Office of Research (June 29, 1992)

League of California Cities, *Making California's Governments Work* (January 1995)

National Association of State Budget Officers, *Budget Processes in the States* (September 1997)

National Conference of State Legislatures, *State Strategies to Manage Budget Shortfalls* (December 1996); *Fundamentals of Sound State Budgeting Practices* (May 1995); *The Performance Budget Revisited: a Report on State Budget Reform* (February 1994)

National Performance Review, From Red Tape to Results: Creating a Government that Works Better & Costs Less (September 7, 1993)

Oregon Progress Board, *Oregon Benchmarks: Standards for Measuring Statewide Progress and Governmental Performance* (December 1992)

Fiscal Federalism Conference, *RAND Research Review, Vol. XX, No. 1* (Summer 1996)

Scott, Steve, "Fiscally Unfit," *California Journal, Vol. XXVIII, No. 9* (September 1997)

Shires, Michael A. and Melissa Glenn Haber, *A Review of Local Government Data in California*, Public Policy Institute of California (February 1997)

Shultz, Jim, *State of Deadlock: A Case Study of the California Budget War*, Advocacy Institute West (February 1993)

Stowers, Genie N.L., "Budgeting in Cyberspace," *Government Finance Review* (February 1998)

Twentieth Century Fund/Century Foundation, *The Basics: Balancing the Budget*, Guide to the Issues (1997)

Vasconcellos, John, *California at the Crossroads: A California Smart Budget Update & Alarm*, Assembly Ways and Means Committee (June 30, 1994)

III. World Wide Web Sites

California Budget Project: http://www.cbp.org

California State Association of Counties: http://csac.counties.org

California Taxpayers' Association: http://www.caltax.org

The Center for the Study of the States, Nelson A Rockefeller Institute of Government:
http://www.crisny.org/business/companies/rockinst/c_stysta.htm

Council of State Governments: http://www.csg.org

Department of Finance: http://www.dof.ca.gov

Legislative Analyst's Office: http://www.lao.ca.gov

National Association of State Budget Officers: http://www.nasbo.org

National Conference of State Legislatures: http://www.ncsl.org

Public Policy Institute of California: http://www.ppic.org

RAND: http://www.rand.org

State Assembly: http://www.assembly.ca.gov

State Senate: http://www.sen.ca.gov

Notes: